LIBERATING
LEADERSHIP

BEING NO ONE

HAVING NOTHING

GOING NOWHERE

INCLUDING

101

Leadership
NUDGES

LIBERATING
LEADERSHIP

Being No One
Having Nothing
Going Nowhere

Everyone's Leadership Journey!

Mike George

Gavisus Media

Liberating Leadership

Text Copyright Mike George 2018

Print Edition ISBN: 978-0-9933877-6-0

Also available as an E-Book

Published by
Gavisus Media

Email: gavisusmedia@gmail.com

First Edition
The moral rights of the author have been asserted.

Cover Design: Charlotte Mouncey - www.bookstyle.co.uk

Other Books by Mike George

The Wisdom of Personal Undevelopment
The Art of Liberation by Unlearning and Undoing

BEING BEYOND BELIEF
How to KNOW what is TRUE for YOU!

MINDSETS
Changing your perception and creating new perspectives

The 7 Myths About LOVE...Actually!
The Journey from Your HEAD to the HEART of Your SOUL

BEING Your Self
SEEing and KNOWing What's IN the Way IS the Way!

Don't Get MAD Get Wise
Why no one ever makes you angry...ever!

The Immune System of the SOUL
Freeing Your Self from ALL Forms of Dis - ease

The Journey from IGNORANCE to ENIGHTENMENT
The only journey where you are guaranteed to lose all your baggage.

The 7 AHA!s of Highly Enlightened Souls
How to Free YOUR Self from ALL Forms of Stress

Learn to Find Inner Peace
Manage your anxieties, think well, feel well.

Learn to Relax
Ease tension, conquer stress and free the self

In the Light of Meditation
A guide to meditation and spiritual awakening

———————————

Subscribe to CLEAR THINKING

Clear Thinking is a regularly irregular e-article that serves to sustain the ongoing unlearning necessary to increase your self - awareness and self - understanding - to subscribe, go to www.relax7.com.

Authentic leaders are seldom seen
in the spotlight of fame.
They are the unknown heroes
who quietly show others the way
by their action, by their attitude,
by their presence.

Their touch is light,
their nature gentle,
their wisdom deep,
their authenticity and
their strength of character
evident when those around them
believe there is a crisis.

They would not consider
themselves to be a leader.
They do not seek to be
'the leader'.
Yet they are held
in the vision of others
as someone from whom to
'take a lead'.

CONTENTS

"Even when
you
are not formally recognized as
'the leader'
and you live mostly
in an informal context,
you
are still leading,
simply because
there is
always someone
watching...

...and when there isn't,
you are!

BEING a Leader and DOING Leadership

Leadership is contextual. You will lead others differently if you are in a commercial organisation than you would in a community. You will develop different leadership styles if you are a parent or a writer or a care worker. You would call on different leadership skills as a teacher than you would as an engineer or a midwife. Yet they are all leadership roles. Every role is potentially a leadership role, as there is almost always someone alongside you in any given scene!

Most of the thousands of leadership books and programmes currently on offer tend to narrow their focus to the attributes and competencies necessary to lead in a commercial, business-management context. Perhaps that's because it's where the money is in leadership coaching, teaching and workshopping. Yet few highlight the fact that leadership is 'context dependent'. The context common to all our lives is relationship. Of this we have no choice. Which means we are all leaders for someone, somewhere at some moments in time. That's why the thread that runs through becoming and being a leader, in any context, is 'authenticity of character'.

A leadership 'strategy' only comes into play when there is a clear 'collective' objective. It will be defined by *where* 'we' want to go, *what* 'we' want to achieve and even *why* 'we' want to get there. But crucially, 'the *how*' will always depend on 'character'.

The shaping of our character depends largely on the nature of our conditioning. While we may have received a deep and profound wisdom from those around us as we grew up, it can never be our own wisdom. We have undoubtedly inherited and assimilated many illusions and misbeliefs from our culture, education and parental influences. Unfortunately, for most of us, it's such illusions and delusions that will shape our character, influence our decisions, guide our behaviours and dictate our destiny.

That's why there has to be a 'spectrum of context' in any understanding of what it means to be a leader. From the inner, invisible context of consciousness, where character is created and shaped each day, to the outer, visible behaviours in the context of groups, organisations and commercial enterprises. From the invisible states of consciousness that shape practical visible skills and abilities; from our invisible thoughts and feelings that will visibly influence how well we connect with others; from our invisible perceptions that will hinder or help how effectively we will visibly practice the art of persuasion; from our invisible attitudes that will influence our visible behaviours; from our own invisible self-mastery that will give us the ability to guide others to be the masters of their 'self'.

It's clear that the foundations for the ability to lead in any external situation begins with the internal and invisible movements of consciousness itself.

While this may appear obvious to some it is often not fully recognized in leadership development programmes. Yes, there has been an increasing investment in emotional mastery; there is a growing emphasis on the cultivation of intuition; there is an interest in spiritual intelligence; even morality and ethics have become part of the leaders education. But the commercialisation of such topics and the competitive context in which they are applied, has tended to dilute the truths required for a deeper understanding and effective practice. Spirituality is still largely an avoided concept in business while morality and ethics tend to be perceived as necessary 'add ons'.

But character cannot be shaped well or indeed repaired or, as some would suggest, rediscovered, unless such aspects of our consciousness, such aspects of 'the invisible', are brought into the light of our own awareness. Only then can we stop sabotaging our own character and recover what is often referred to as our 'true nature'.

BEING a Leader

Being a leader begins with how we create our states of being. The first part of this book looks at the mistakes we have been taught to make which distort our states and thereby diminish our character, ensuring authenticity will be elusive if not impossible. We investigate the three primary illusions that we all learn, regardless of culture or upbringing, which will not allow us to remain aligned to the truth of who 'I am' nor be authentic in our relationships with others.

DOING Leadership

The second part visits the other end of the 'spectrum of context' suggesting specific actions you can take, from inside-out and outside-in, to enhance you leadership competencies in an organisational context.

Leadership skills, competencies, attributes and qualities are not difficult to identify and talk about. But embodying and demonstrating such skills consistently, depends entirely on your personal level of authenticity, your willingness to practice and to what extent you are the master of your consciousness. One of the reasons it's hard to change the habits of a lifetime is our unawareness of the deeper origins of our habits. Original causes are hard to 'see'. The integration of Parts One and Two provide invitations to experiment, test, succeed and learn and unlearn from frequent failure! In that process you will 'see'.

Part One enlightens your awareness while Part Two suggests situations and scenarios where you can make that gradual enlightenment visible, thereby accelerating the creation of your leadership competencies.

Leadership – The Spectrum of Context

INTERNAL Where character is shaped and developed		EXTERNAL Where character shapes behaviour
Are you the master (leader) of all the creative processes within your consciousness (self) i.e. of your thoughts, feelings, attitudes, decisions and perceptions? In other words, have you freed your self from ALL your conditioning?	As you bring the internal out into the external through whatever role you may play (manager, parent, engineer, midwife, teacher etc.) is the authenticity of your character coming through the skills that you practice? Even saying and doing nothing, at the 'appropriate' moments, is an attribute of leadership.	Are you able to be consistently proactive, caring and helpful towards ALL others while ensuring the task is done? Do people perceive you are authentic and that your character is consistently worthy of respect and trust?

The Invisible Journey

There are two journeys in life. One is visible and the other is invisible. One is called 'making your way' in the world and the other is 'knowing the way' within your consciousness. The first is compulsory and the second tends to be either ignored or neglected; it's validity often denied.

Only when you 'know the way' within your consciousness can you rediscover and 'be' the authentic you. Only then can you 'liberate' your natural abilities and the accurate character traits to lead others.

Each of us has the opportunity to make both these journeys. The first journey is the manifest, visible, 'never a dull moment' journey 'out there'. The second is internal and invisible, with 'many a quiet reflective moment', in here!

Unfortunately, most of us do not recognise the significance of the second, while many will not even acknowledge there is such a journey.

> **By the way...**
> Is your life a good example? Is the way you live your life something others could take a lead from? Are you speaking and acting in ways that would be an inspiration for others? Are you guiding, teaching, counselling, facilitating, coaching, mentoring or just helping others, in any way? If so, you are a leader.

Deeper Dimensions

The inner journey requires digging deeply into consciousness with a curiosity and fascination that reveals what consciousness is exactly, how it works precisely, why everything you do originates there and therefore its role in your daily life.

Understanding consciousness is the same as understanding your self. While it's not part of our formal or informal education, it's also not rocket science. From the moment we arrive, to the moment we venture out into the big wide world, no one helps us to understand how we, as conscious beings or beings of consciousness, actually work.

Yet it's within our consciousness that everything in our life will occur. We have learned to believe that other people and events occur only 'out there'. But no one teaches us why or how we create our own version of everyone and everything that we encounter out there, 'in here'.

By the way...

There are many teachers, presenters and writers who talk about the importance of self-awareness and self-mastery in the context of leadership development. But it seems few place the inner journey front and center in whatever way they package their advice, guidance, techniques and methods.

Follow the Trail

To many of us it's now obvious that the state of our world reflects a crisis in leadership in almost every context from politics to business, from health care to social cohesion, from the environment to our climate. This, in turn, is simply a reflection of a crisis of human intelligence, which is a crisis of consciousness, which is rooted in a lack of understanding of our self.

The visible machinations of human behavior have their roots in the invisible states of human consciousness itself. Self, intelligence, spirit and consciousness are essentially describing the same thing which, in the simplest of terms, is the 'I' that says 'I am'. The self is conscious, so you and I are consciousness, we are intelligent, so you and I are intelligence itself. Only words seem to create a separation of ideas.

It's a Mess

So, if the world is in a bit of a mess, generally speaking, it just means we are in a bit of a mess, generally speaking! I don't mean mess as in a dark and negative sense. More in a confused, dazed, sleepy, there is some 'chaos in consciousness', sense.

Even when we think our life is in order and we have built our personalized comfort zones, there is still some chaos, there is still some messiness 'in here'! If we 'insperience' any suffering, sorrow or stress, there is some messiness in our consciousness. However, for many of us, our physical comforts assuage our sufferings and stressful feelings. At the same time our ego maintains our apparent cleverness as we keep our mental and emotional chaos either at bay or at tolerable levels. Most of the time.

But that just ensures we remain unaware of our confusions or we suppress our inner messiness or we just live in denial. Perhaps all three! Hence the explosive growth of the therapy industries in the last two decades. But it is undoubtedly our inner chaos and messiness that sabotages our authenticity and diminishes our character.

Yes, there is a tremendous energetic creativity that is being expressed by many people in the world and in our communities. But to what ends? With what intention? Taking us in what direction? These are the deeper questions we don't take time to consider ...so much. They require a clarity and patience that seems to be fast disappearing from our deliberations and conversations.

Are we fully anticipating and allowing for the unintended consequences of our sparkling new technologies? Obviously not. Does our economic philosophy still work in a world where the environment itself contains the ultimate wealth that maintains our health and wellbeing? Obviously not. How does 'entropy' affect the energy of human consciousness? No one seems to ask such a question. What is the destination of a world bewitched and bewildered by social media? The answers, which we now see on a daily basis, include fake news, self-isolation and delicate levels of self-esteem in new generations.

What's really going on?

However, it seems an increasing number of people are interested in understanding their messiness i.e. their stress, their suffering, their unhappiness. More of us are arriving at our 'something isn't right' moment. What is not so apparent is that the process of repairing our consciousness i.e. our self, and therefore the world, is NOT one of learning i.e. absorbing more information and ideas, theories and concepts. It's that particular form of education, which we so highly value, defend and sustain, that has brought us to this point of external and internal messiness.

Only when that is fully recognized, understood and accepted does it becomes fairly obvious that our solutions lie through a process of liberating our self from the illusions and consequent delusions we have already absorbed along the way.

In other words, perhaps it's time to start consciously living from inside out and not outside in. Perhaps it's time to start 'educing' our own wisdom from inside out, and stop blindly consuming so much information from outside in.

The exact same applies to the idea of leadership. Leadership is not so much a process of learning but one of liberation from what has already been learned. Both the authenticity of our character and the character traits we need in order to be both an example and inspiration for others, regardless of the context, are already present within our consciousness.

Restoring and revealing them however, does not require an investment in learning and development but a divestment of much of what we have learned and developed so far. The characteristics of leadership are liberated not learned. The character of the authentic leader is revealed more than redeemed. It is a result of unlearning and undevelopment, not more learning and development.

But these are not ideas that are easily realized or accepted. So much is still invested in the old education and learning paradigm. They may even sound like just another theory, another philosophy, captured by words and concepts on the pages of yet another leadership book.

So, I invite you to sit back, be prepared to be challenged by some radical insights and perhaps a whole new understanding of your self, as we explore what it means to be an authentic human being and therefore an authentic leader.

Whether you occupy a formal leadership position or you're simply making your way through life, the 'inner journey' and the expansion of self-awareness is the same for everyone.

The Ending of Pretending

Did you know you are a pretender? You've been pretending all your life. It's what we are all taught to do. It seems only a few catch-on to the reality that almost everyone is pretending to be someone they are not. It's killing us and it's killing the world. But we can't see it.

It's only in realizing your own pretentiousness that you can help others to liberate themselves from its many constraints. When your pretentiousness is no more then you fulfill the oldest description of leadership, which is 'being an example' of exemplary behavior.

It's not what you say, it's what you do. It's what's both visible and invisible in your deeds that touches and inspires others, or not, as the case may be.

This is only possible when you stop doing what you were previously not aware you were doing i.e. pretending to be someone you are not, pretending you have something, which you don't, pretending you are going somewhere significant, which you can't. Only then can you be authentic. It's that authenticity that shows up in your character and it's your 'character' that arises out of your authenticity. Only then are you a magnetic example for others.

In this first part we focus on understanding the various pretenses that we all learn and how they shape our entire life. Plus the practices necessary to shake off our pretentiousness! For many these will be radical insights and not for the faint hearted. Although, there's a good chance they may also trigger some light heartedness! Fully realizing for your self that you are no one, that you have nothing and that you are going nowhere, is transformational. But a book can only put up signposts. Only you can induce the realization of such realities for your self, within your self.

That's not to say, that once you have realized, you just give up and lay down and do nothing for the rest of your days. On the contrary, quite the opposite. You will be both motivated and able to *do* much more and *be* much more effective in the process. You will *feel* freer, and that elusive sense of fulfillment and satisfaction will come to visit more often. What you be and do with your life is likely to be different from what you are 'being' and 'doing' right now. But then again, maybe not!

As you explore and experiment with the **101 Leadership Nudges** in the second part of the book, you start to walk parallel tracks.

In the background of your consciousness you will have these three profound but expanding ideas of being no one, having nothing and going nowhere, while being challenged, as a leader, to navigate and improve your everyday world of human interactions. In that process you 'may' see why believing you *are* someone and *have* something get in the way of your ability to be authentic and how they compromise your leadership style.

> **By the way...**
> Do you ever get the feeling you just want to ignore the status quo? Something arises inside you that says, "What on earth is going on, what are we doing, where is everyone going, why are people so...?
>
> These questions are often the signs you have become aware that large parts of the game of life 'out there' has become a pretense.
>
> There are those who sense this from a young age. In the conformists eyes such people seem to act rather strangely. They often become the non-conformist, the eccentric, the rebel in the pack. While the rest of us wonder, "What is the matter with them? Why can't they just be normal and 'fit in' like the rest of us?"
>
> But, for the rebel, fitting in and just pretending with everyone else just doesn't cut the mustard. Such rebels are often unsung leaders.

On the other hand, you may not want to walk and move between these two parallel worlds - the inner and the outer. It may be just too big a gap to bridge. In which case, you have two options. You can either ignore the first part of the book and just get on with the challenges in the second part. Or you could gift the book to someone whom you sense may appreciate this approach.

I would be the first to say it's not easy to bring these two aspects, the inner and the outer, together. It takes time and attention, patience and perseverance, rehearsal and practice. It certainly could not be billed as a quick fix or the 'latest' trend in leadership development.

However, you may start to see exactly how believing you 'are' someone, believing you 'have' something and believing you are 'going' somewhere, are all illusions i.e. beliefs that sabotage your character and therefore your leadership capabilities during the process of interacting with others. But joining these dots will require your abiding interest and curiosity.

I've been sending the nudges in part two weekly to people who have been on leadership retreats and courses for almost 3 years now. It's a way of helping them sustain the momentum of putting 'insight into practice'. What I have not told them is why these suggestions are so difficult to embody, why all leadership competencies are not so easy to practice and why these three beliefs, that we all absorb as we grow up, are what's in the way of their motivation and effort.

These inner and outer journeys represent a challenging juxtaposition between the reality of your inner life and the practicality of your outer activities.

But how…

Whenever I give a talk or workshop on anything to do with self-transformation or consciousness change, one of the most common questions is, "But how do I do it? How do I make this practical?" The answer is, "I don't know how you will do it. That's up to you". If you ask me, "How do I ride a bike, how do I do it?". I can spend hours explaining the theory and describing the actions, but can you then ride a bike competently? No. Only by getting on the bike, trying to ride it and then falling off, probably many times, then solving the 'falling off' problem for your self, do you become a master bike rider. Then it's something you will never forget.

Similarly, even when you start to realize you are, in truth, 'no one' and that in truth, you 'have nothing', and that you are truly 'not going' anywhere, you will likely forget the theory. You may even think, "I don't like those ideas!". Especially as you engage with the demands of the position you occupy, the relationships around you, the bills you have to pay, and all the other things you do to fulfill your responsibilities.

But when you do begin to realize for your self, and then actualize such insights/realizations through your behaviors in the practical reality of your daily life, you begin to slowly shape and live your life quite differently. But it's not up to me or anyone else to tell you how that will be or how that 'should' look to others.

In the world of action and reaction the application of a theory can be awkward and tense, as mistakes are inevitably made. In the universe of consciousness, the application of a realization is also awkward at first, simply because there are already beliefs and habits installed in consciousness, in you, that contradict the realization. If you realize peacefulness is your true nature it may take a little while for that to be a consistent state of being, as you've been busy creating states of stress and peacelessness all your life. They have become established habits.

Between HERE, which is where you are now i.e. believing you are somebody and/or wanting to be somebody, and THERE, where you've fully realized and re-awoken to the reality that you are no one and have nothing, there are likely to be a few bumps on the road, a few obstacles and perhaps the occasional bruised feeling, metaphorically speaking, along the way. And that is as it should be. How often did you fall off your bike, how much pain and how many scabbed knees were you prepared to take on the road to mastery?

The price of liberation, like the price of mastery, is often a little discomfort. We've already made our selves comfortable with our current levels of discomfort! We settle easily for our stress and unhappiness, believing they are a natural part of how life works. In the process of realizing these three radical truths for your self it's highly likely there will be moments when you accentuate your own discomfort and stress. But such periods will pass as you gradually see and know with greater clarity.

I don't get it!

You may also find your self thinking, "What is this guy talking about?" or perhaps "There is no way this is true for me", or perhaps, "This is an impossible mindset to bring to the practical realities of my relationships at work in my daily life", or perhaps "I just don't know how to apply this".

Perfectly natural thoughts, which will arise simply because your 'conditioning' says the opposite, people around you say and live the opposite, while the world at large operates with the opposite mindset. These resistant thoughts are also the early equivalent of trying to find balance on your bike. In such moments, it pays to remind your self, that ALL your stress/suffering/unhappiness arises from the 'ideas' that you are someone or should be someone, that you have something/s or should have more somethings and that you are going somewhere significant in your life.

It pays to revisit these insights as often as possible, perhaps every day to start with. Remind your self. See for your self. Understand for your self. And as you input into your consciousness that kind of information from the pages of a book i.e. from 'outside in', gradually the realization of such inner realities will start to arise from 'inside out'.

That's because, deep down, you already know.

Part ONE

The Inner Journey

Revelations and Realizations on the Way Back to Authenticity

Preparing for Your Journey

We begin with our three radical insights. Might it be accurate to say that the only truly authentic people, and therefore authentic leaders, are those that have realized and live by three basic truths?

I am no one

I have nothing

I am going nowhere

It turns out that not only are such people often more capable of showing and teaching others 'the way', they are more likely to be the embodiment of the way.

The way to where? To nowhere! How so? Step right this ...way!

To most people, being no one, having nothing and going nowhere will sound strange, off the wall, possibly off the planet. While it applies to every single human being, as I'll attempt to demonstrate, it is more than challenging to pragmatic leaders of organizations/teams/groups, parents of families and ordinary people who consider themselves members of all kinds of communities, up and down the land.

To some it may sound too esoteric, to others it reminds them of the belief system of some religio-spiritual philosophy. And to a few it's more like the practice of some ascetic in a mountain cave. They certainly sound like ideas that are not appropriate to the ambitious, hi-tech, fast changing, constantly demanding, materially focused, commercial landscape of the modern organization in the modern world.

So, I am going to set out before you exactly why, even in such a pragmatic context as our complex, uncertain, yet highly organized, material world, these three insights into the reality of human consciousness are the basis for the only authentic way to create a meaningful and happy life, while being an example for others.

Leaders all

Whether you are a parent, friend, manager, colleague, brother or sister, we are all leaders. There is always someone watching your behavior, sensing your attitude, listening to your words. We are all leaders, perhaps not by position or qualification, but by attitude and action. Perhaps not all the time. But during your life there will be many moments when you care, nurture, connect and influence others. Or just one other. It doesn't really matter how often or for what reason.

What matters is that whenever you are in the company of others, implicit in any gathering, there is the opportunity to demonstrate the attributes and competencies of leadership. The only prerequisite is the acknowledgment and acceptance of complete responsibility for your self, which means 'everything' you think, feel and do.

Sounds easy and perhaps obvious, but in most cultures today, it is not a well-practiced ethic. We tend to be conditioned by our upbringing, education and surrounding culture, to blame, complain and criticize. In other words, be a 'projector of responsibility' onto someone else or some event/circumstance.

Consensus leadership profile

Before we begin our journey it's worth reminding our self of the commonly acknowledged descriptive profile of an effective leader and therefore, what many may call 'someone of good character'.

Imagine you are an excellent leader and therefore an excellent attitudinal and behavioral example for others. What would that look like. What would others see, feel, receive, come to know, about you?

Take a moment. Close the book and ...imagine! Visualize a brilliant example of leadership. Build a profile. Remember, whatever you can imagine, you can do! Relax and paint a picture in your mind.

Then resume reading.

Might such a profile look something like this?

You give **RESPECT** and regard to everyone you meet, regardless of their history or the history of your relationship with them. That's easy, isn't it?

You always **CELEBRATE** the success and achievements of others, as you genuinely want to see others do well. You do, don't you?

You always **ENCOURAGE** others, with your effervescent enthusiasm, to be the best of themselves in their life. Every day, right?

You are always **AVAILABLE** when others need someone to listen to their story or guide them forward through a difficult situation, even when you are not feeling too good yourself. Aren't you, always?

You are frequently looking for ways to **ELEVATE** others by often putting them ahead of your self. You step back a lot, don't you?

You are always **LISTENING** before speaking and listening not just to the words of others but to their deepest feelings. What have you learned to hear?

You are always able to **EMPATHISE** with others as they go through different challenges and occasional crisis. Or do you also lose the emotional plot alongside them, thinking that that is what supports them?

You are able to **TRUST** everyone and they feel trustworthy in your presence because you've realized no one can hurt you. Elementary, isn't it?

You are always **OPEN** to others point of view, their position, perceptions and desires. Always willing to discuss and dialogue. You never argue, do you?

You **NURTURE** the growing experience of others as you help them to nurture their own talents and capabilities. Of course you do!

You are a **KIND** and generous person who always enquires as to the wellbeing and needs of the other and, where possible, meet their needs. Every time, right?

You are always **ACCEPTING** of others point of view, their state of being, their behaviors - without necessarily agreeing or condoning. You never resist others, do you?

You always hold out the hand of **CO-OPERATION** as you step forward to help, when help is obviously required. At every opportunity, yes?

You have infinite **PATIENCE** with everyone as you know some need more time and attention than others to grow and develop. Or do you agitate when the clock is running down?

You are always **PROACTIVE** as you focus on solutions and not problems and you are always seeking new ways to improve. Undoubtedly so, yes?

You always speak openly and **HONESTLY** when it is required to inform others exactly what you think and feel. You are consistent in this, si?

Just some of characteristics you might find within a consensus profile of a leader. There are probably many more. Add your own.

At this point you might be thinking, "But this is the profile of a saint!" And that's true. Certainly, in their full measure. But ask anyone to write down a profile of the character traits of a leader and most if not all of the above would probably be mentioned.

When written like this, such attributes appear to be separate. But in real life they flow and merge into one another making combinations that are unique to each individual. Much depends on how you perceive, interpret and respond to whoever and whatever is in front of you.

Natural Expression of Authenticity

They are not traits or abilities that are unique to a few. They are not skills or even competencies. They are the natural characteristics of a someone who is being authentic while in the presence of others.

They are not 'learned' so you cannot be trained to demonstrate such attributes genuinely. They emerge naturally from someone who is simply being their natural self. Which is the same as to say such traits and behaviors won't be real when you are being inauthentic in any way.

As a consequence there are just two big questions that arise

Why can't you bring such characteristics to the party as much as you'd like and deploy them ...appropriately? Why can't you be and do any of the above ...consistently? If you can't, appropriately and consistently, it means there is an absence of authenticity.

In other words, why can't you make this kind of 'ideal' in theory, 'real' in your practice?

Three reasons:

> You believe you are somebody
>
> You believe you are in possession of some things
>
> You believe you are going somewhere

When you hold such beliefs, the consequences are twofold.

1 You start to have an 'agenda' in your interactions with others. With some more than others. Perhaps you have a position to protect or that you want to accentuate. Perhaps you want more 'things' because they represent security, success or comfort, so there is 'stuff' that needs to be acquired and possessed. Perhaps your ambitions mean you often believe you need to get ahead or stay ahead of someone else.

2 You start to create emotions such as fear, sadness and anger. Fear of losing what you believe you already have. Sadness following any loss (all loss is inevitable to someone who believes they possess). And anger, as you look for someone or some event on which to project blame for your loss. Often your imagination is enough to generate such emotional states.

It's both the agenda you carry into your relationships and the various forms of these emotions that not only constitute stress and suffering, they sabotage your ability to make the highest ideals consistently real. They dilute authenticity.

Fork in the Road

When you genuinely ask yourself, "Why can I not be consistent in bringing such character traits to the reality of day-to-day life?", you may start to see a fork in the road ahead. Down the left fork is learning and development and down the right fork is unlearning and undevelopment.

The vast majority will head down the left-hand fork believing that we need to learn and develop such attributes. Have you ever been on a leadership, management or personal development course? Have you ever sent someone on such a course? Why? Primarily, it's the illusion that the character traits in our profile are simply skills and competences that can be learned. Just like we used to learn things at school. Or believe we did! That kind of learning requires teachers and teachers earn money from teaching so there is a business that can be built out of teaching in what is now known as the field of 'learning and development'. It becomes the mission of such teachers, and the organizations that they establish, to sustain the illusion that such 'attributes of character' can be learned and developed.

Few will set off down the other path of unlearning and undevelopment. That's usually because it seems only a few fully understand that such characteristics arise naturally from the restoration of a clear and free state of being. Few realize such attributes cannot be learned. Only rediscovered, reclaimed, reinvigorated aspects of the inner landscape of consciousness itself. Not the result of 'adding to' (learning) but the outcome of 'taking away' (unlearning), of releasing all that is in the way of the natural expression of such attributes within consciousness.

It's in the process of dispelling the illusions that you are someone, that you have something and that you are going somewhere, that the attributes, capabilities and qualities within our vision of the authentic leader are then seen, known and felt to be already present within each and every one of us.

This is why leadership is liberated and not learned.

Pie in the sky?

But just before we proceed there may be a few, perhaps more than a few, who would posit that leadership is as much driven by the angry, forceful, stressed out, dictator manager/parent. That it's the person with the most ruthless, aggressive, ambitious and manipulative character that dominates others in order to get them to do what the aggressor wants. Many believe that is the way to get ahead.

A few obviously do get away with being and acting in such ways. Usually because they work in the formal context of an organization. That's a place where you most often don't get to choose the people you work with or choose those who would be your manager/leader. Neither do children get to choose their parents.

But if you had a choice would you choose to work under or be brought up by the shouty, aggressive, manipulative, non-trusting person? Or would you prefer the person characterized by the traits in our profile at the start of the chapter? Does the shouty, aggressive, manipulative, non-trusting person go on courses where they are taught to become angry, stressed, grumpy, aggressive and belligerent managers? Don't think so!

While the shouty, aggressive, manipulative, non-trusting person may rise in their position within the formal context of their organization would you call them successful? Their behaviors are obviously expressions of their own internal, self-created unhappiness. Would we call that successful?

While our profile of the character traits of a leader may seem pie in the sky and not always to be found in many organizations and even families, they are what we recognize, value and aspire to. They are what we would hope for and expect of someone playing a leadership role in any context/relationship.

So, let's get to the heart of what is in the way within each and every one of us being able to consistently and authentically demonstrate such traits. The internal obstacles and barriers are the same for all of us. We have all learned to assimilate the same illusions.

It's these three illusions, call them beliefs if you like, that are also responsible for all human suffering, stress, conflict and war in our world, near and far.

Believing I am someone (the desire to be somebody significant)

Believing I have some things (the desire to acquire 'more')

Believing I am going somewhere (the desire to go places)

Only by fully understanding why and how such beliefs distort your character and ensure you misuse your energy in the context of all your relationships can you:

a) restore your authenticity.

b) free your self from your agendas.

c) end the habit of creating emotional disturbances within your consciousness i.e. suffering and stress.

d) make the ideal real in natural and easy ways.

BEING NO ONE

...and the Art of Being Self-less

*"Have you ever had the sense of watching your self doing something?
Even while you're speaking, even while you're thinking. Somehow 'you'
are watching your self speaking and thinking and doing. The one who
is watching, who is aware of being the watcher, is you. The real you.
Not the you that you 'think' or 'say' you are! Not the you that you've
been taught to believe you are. When you cultivate this
'observational awareness' you come to realize the
immense freedom of being no one
and just ...watching".*

Being no one does not mean you do not exist. When you realize you are no one, existence becomes richer and more colorful. Being no one does not mean life becomes meaningless. There arises both the realization that you create your own meaning and an increased capacity to be a maker of 'accurate meaning'. Being no one does not mean you abandon family and friends. You will have a deeper level of intimacy and connection with everyone in your circle when you fully realize you, and 'they', are no one! Being no one does not mean you wander the world searching for an identity. You have no identity. It was not lost. You cannot lose what was not there in the first place. Your 'worldly identities' are necessary, but they are not you. When you 'know' this to be true, you can more playfully engage in and with the world, because you no longer expect it to give you, and affirm for you, a sense of 'who I am'.

Strange idea this; being no one. But it's what you already are and forever will be. This is why!

The ideal and the real

Most of us believe we need to become and be someone. We believe it's right to aspire and strive to be somebody in the eyes of others. It's a common belief that success in life happens only when you are recognized by others as 'somebody of achievement'. Some already believe they are someone special, someone famous, a great achiever, a hard worker, a clever person, a brilliant leader.

Here is the crux of the matter; attempting to 'be', and maintain 'being a belief' about your self, means you cannot be your 'self'.

You are trying to be (live up to) a belief, and you are not a belief. A belief is an idea, or a set of ideas, forming a concept. You are not an idea. If you try to be an idea, sometimes known 'the ideal', it means you cannot be authentic, you cannot be 'real'. Pursuing an ideal ensures you will miss the real. In the context of your character there is a paradox. To be real it is necessary to stop trying to be the ideal and only then does the ideal emerge naturally to become real!

In other words, don't 'try' to be caring and kind, empathic and open. 'Trying to be' such traits, which is the almost same is 'learning to develop', is pursuing an ideal. You will be naturally caring and kind, naturally open and empathic, when you stop 'trying to be' a caring, kind, open and empathic person just because you 'believe you should or want to be'! Such traits emerge naturally when you are being your authentic self. When you try to 'become the ideal' you will miss the real.

We tend to be conditioned to believe we 'have to become' what we are taught to believe we 'should become'. Somebody! In this instance, the caring, kind, open and empathic 'ideas' are combined to form an image of the 'ideal somebody'. Trying to be that somebody means you will forget how to be your self. Subtle, isn't it. But not so subtle as to interfere detrimentally with the entire course of your inner and outer life.

On entry into the world

From the day you arrive you are told who you are according to: where you arrived, with whom you grow up, what you do, what you look like, the clan you belong to, the tribe you affiliate with and what you should believe. But none of those are who you are. They are simply ideas and concepts, and you and I are not ideas and concepts. As a result, when we identify our self with any of them we learn to be inauthentic. But we are unaware of our inauthenticity. We learn to create an inauthentic character without being aware we do so.

Character comes from consciousness. Unfortunately, we are not taught what consciousness is. Only that we are conscious. We are not taught how to create our 'state of consciousness' i.e. our state of being. We mistakenly learn that our state being is shaped by external forces such as situations, events and other people. We are 'told', mostly, what kind of thoughts and feelings we 'should' have. Most of the feelings we are taught to have and that are generally approved off, are simply emotional states that rise and fall and depend on some trigger stimulation from outside in.

> **By the way...**
> Some people use other words for consciousness e.g. soul, spirit, psyche or just self. All refer to the energy of the 'I' that says 'I am'. As opposed to the energy of form or the body that is animated and occupied by consciousness. Your brain is an aspect of form, it is not what you are!

Who YOU Really Are

It only takes a few moments of reflection and awareness to realize consciousness is what I/you/we each are. You are conscious, therefore you are consciousness. Yes, I've made what is a verb (being conscious) into a noun (consciousness) and applied it to you/me/us. For you, as you read this 'information', that might just sound like someone else's belief. But for many, perhaps not so many, they don't believe it, they 'know', consciousness is what they are.

It is within consciousness that words and concepts are created. We then use such words to 'describe' where we arrive, when we are born, what kind of clan/race we are born into, what we do, where we work, what we are named and the kind of form we occupy. The key word is 'description'. Language describes. It is the bridge between consciousness and the material world around us. Non-physical thought becomes language and language becomes physical sound.

Unfortunately, the primary shaper of our character becomes a sense of identity based on a description. That's when we give birth to the ego. The simplest definition of ego is *a false sense of self.* If you learn to believe you are what you do, where you come from, your race, your belief system, etc., you have learned to identify with a description, with an idea/s. You learn to build your identity using words and the ideas that the words describe, and with the images the words invoke in your own mind. But you and I, we are not descriptions, we are not ideas, we are not images, we are the creators and sustainers of words and ideas.

But if you believe you are what has been used to describe you then whenever someone says something against or descriptively criticizes that description of you, then you suffer. You create suffering for your self within your self. If you lose your job (described set of activities), and therefore the job title (status description) that you have learned to identify your self with, then you make your self suffer by creating sorrow, and perhaps anger, in your consciousness.

You'd rather not suffer so you start to defend, hold on, become protectively attached to the various descriptions of you that you use to create an identity. That's when you create fear in the form of anxiety and insecurity within your consciousness. Those become habitual creations and it's those habits that sabotage your character. That's why you cannot be authentic when you identify with what is not you. And everything in not you!

Reality says that any and all descriptions can be insulted or attacked or lost at any moment. That's why we become anxious. We have no control over when and how that may happen. If you are 'out there' somewhere in the space called social media it means you have created and projected images and ideas about who you 'believe' you are. One minor insult or not enough 'likes' seems to ruin some people's days. Why? Because they believe they are a description!

It's not so easy to see this after a lifetime of 'conditioning'. But if you start to see this you are standing at the threshold of your freedom. Otherwise you are trapped in the ideas and concepts that form what you might consider as your reputation. Are you a reputation? In the universe of consciousness a reputation is a concept which is a thing. Are you a 'thing'? Or are no thing! Not nothing. But not a thing!

Notice how some people suffer with bouts of anger and indignation when their reputation, which they believe is what they are, does not even register and be recognized in the minds of others. "Don't you know who I am?", says the famous celebrity/guru frustratingly and expectantly, as he tries to get a table at a busy restaurant.

So, when you build your identity out of any 'description' you will inevitably create these habits of fear, anxiety, anger and sadness. Such habits ensure your character becomes diminished, distorted, dysfunctional, dependent and often just ...daft! Not necessarily in that order and not necessarily all at once!

Stop, Look, See for your Self

Take a moment to reflect on your character now. Be honest. Do you ever become regularly anxious? Are you ever upset? Are you moody at any time? Do you act selfishly, ever? Are you afraid of losing ...anything? Do you experience all of the above, and more ...frequently?

If you do then see if you can 'see' that the root cause is 'always' the illusion that you are being someone, or trying to be somebody, that you are not!

Yes? We all do this to various degrees. It's what we are taught. But that is not to say it's normal. It's just what we have all learned to create. Whenever we identify with a description and/or the objects of such descriptions, we make a mistake. Suffering is the clue such a mistake is being made. But it's just a mistake.

You might then say, "Well that's what the whole world does". To which I might say, "Yes, that's probably true, but that's why almost everyone is asleep. That's why we often applaud someone who has a character that is non-defensive, non-protecting, non-dependent, not distorted i.e. open, honest, transparent, unaffected by the slings and arrows of other's criticisms or the subjective loss of the objects that the descriptions represent. They stand out. Their ability to respond in wise and appropriate ways to people and circumstances touch us deeply and we may even say, "They are so authentic".

It's also why leadership is now a multi-billion Dollar, Yen, Euro industry. It's an industry that focusses largely on 'character remediation'. That's also a mistake. Yes, it's often called skill development, or fulfilling your potential or empowering your self or identifying your key performance indicators.

But scratch the surface of all those 'terms' (descriptions!) and you'll likely find an attempt at 'character remediation'. And that's what you don't need to do. Your natural character and all its natural traits is already there, within you. But it's only accessible when you realize who you are. Which is accompanied by realizing and dissolving ideas about who you are not.

Strip away all the descriptions, all the ideas, and what are you left with? No one! The restoration and revelation of 'authentic character' is a natural by-product of realizing you are no one. But don't tell Hollywood! It's probably the ultimate paradox, in linguistic terms at least – to be who you really are it's necessary to realize you are no one!

Being who you are ...already!

Come with me for a moment. See if this sounds right and feels right to you. Within you, and within the consciousness of every human being, there is a state of being that is prior to language, prior to ideas and images, prior to the recordings of experiences and memories, prior to who or what you've been taught to 'think' you are.

This state is silent and still. The silence and stillness of consciousness. It's at the core of your being. It 'is' the core of you. Not your body or your brain. But you! It's not separate from you. It is you. It's prior to all the internal noise that we call thoughts and feelings, desires and dreams. Mystics know this state. Many practicing meditators know this state. Highly enlightened beings know this state. It's there, within all of us. It's prior to the creation of all your habits that go to make up your personality, your character type, in this moment.

In this pure state of consciousness, some might call it your original state of being, you have no sense of identity. You don't need one. You are simply being your self. Radiating the energy of your being, your consciousness, you.

That radiation is clear, pure and completely free of any distortion. It's 'natural' because it's arising from your natural state of being. But of course, you cannot stay in that still and silent state because here we are, interrelating, interacting, inter, well everything, in the world of relationship, action and form.

We invent and create language to communicate with each other. No problem. Very creative. You could say very clever. But look at what's happened. We have all learned to believe we are what we use language to describe. We learn to believe we are a description of something other than our self.

Descriptions are always changing because the world of action and form is always changing. What happens when you identify with something that is always changing, always unstable? You start to feel insecure, which is fear; feel anxious, which is fear; feel worried about what will happen, which is fear; feel disappointment when the object you have used to describe you is no longer there, which is sadness. The creating of fear and sadness become habitual and both set up camp in your character. That's why we suffer. Then we project that suffering on to others as we avoid responsibility. That's called ignorance. Not in a negative sense. It's just that we are not aware. Eventually the fear becomes inexplicable panic attacks and the sadness becomes depression. Life becomes a journey into suffering.

The suffering is tolerable until it's not, at which point we go searching for relief, for the antidote, often spurred on by the thought, "There must be something more than a life lived in fear (insecurity) and sadness (depression)". Deep down you know there is. Deep down you have a vague memory of the silence and stillness, of the freedom and radiance, of the clarity and powerfulness, of your natural state of being. The 'authentic you' is prior to all of that 'language based' thinking and talking and doing and identifying.

So, of you go on your workshop, your retreat, your encounter with a wise man or woman, who then proceeds to set up signposts and offers insights into YOU, as they remind you that all you need to do is 'be your self'. "Be what you were and still are, when you were being silent and still". And all they say is, "Go there now!". Go be in that state of being and you will start to see that whatever you describe with words, whatever you identify with, whatever you use to build your sense of self ...IS NOT YOU!

I could go on. But I won't. All I will say is don't just believe this. Go there, be there, know there, and you will start to 'liberate' your true, brilliant, perfected character that was there, is still there, and will forever be there. And, the more you do 'go there', the faster all the unnatural character traits, all the habitually fearful, dependent, distorted, delusional, thoughts and behaviors, atrophy and die. Some not quite so fast!

By the way, when I say, 'go there' it really means 'be here'!

How do you go there? How do you 'be here'. Well 'you' are already there, which is here! But you're not aware of it. So the question is how do you invoke, expand and deepen that awareness? Well you can use some 'practices' such as meditation or deep introspection or quiet but earnest contemplation.

More about 'the practices', or the 'way there', later.

Between There and Here

You cannot 'learn' true character. Take another look at our leader profile again. When you believe that you can learn these attributes you may be able to model the behavior, but if it's not genuinely arising from the authentic you, then it's forced, it's false. And people sense that, they feel it. You sense your own falsity, your own insincerity. Plus, the trait itself, the ability to respond in such a way, will disappear in a flash in any crisis or chaotic situation. Try being kind to others when you are being criticized. Try being creative when someone is threatening your position. Try being compassionate and proactive when someone has just replaced you and taken what you believed was 'my' job.

Try caring for someone because you 'believe' you should. Then watch the difference when you genuinely care about someone not because you 'believe' you should, but because you know it's the natural thing to do. You don't even 'know it' as in 'think it', you just do it! Notice the difference. Do the same with all those other traits in our profile.

You can't force your self to be open with someone. Well you can, but it won't last long. Whereas, when you are genuinely and naturally open with someone for no reason i.e. not because you heard you should be on your training course, it tends to last much longer and go much deeper. It's authentic.

Most leadership development courses or learning processes feature the same character traits in their ideal leader profile. But seldom do people walk away at the end of the course changed and able to demonstrate those attributes consistently. They cannot be 'learned' as in 'added on' to your character.

To be real such traits have to arise from inside out. They have to be felt naturally. And that 'naturality', so to speak, then shapes responsive behavior. And when there is a crisis or chaos then the character traits don't collapse and fall apart. They are solid and consistent. Therefore credible. And that's what touches and inspires people when they are in the presence of someone being their authentic self.

Cultivating character is not a formulaic process, so it's not a skill set that you learn and then add it to your 'armory'. We are all different in that we have different ways of using the power of our consciousness when it's restored to its true and accurate nature. And that's the key. Restore your awareness of your true nature and the ability to express the appropriate character traits follow ...naturally.

No one can teach you that. But they can trigger your memory of the deep states that are prior to all the stuff you've learned and developed up to now. That deep state is the real you. Not the manufactured you that you create using the 'received conditioning' and all those verbal descriptions of you.

I would recommend you don't try to remember all this. In fact, make no effort to remember any of the information in this book. Simply watch what it awakens in you as you read. Or, more accurately, be aware of what you allow to awaken in you as you read this. Don't try to hold on to it. Just feel it. Acknowledge it. Let whatever song (feeling) grow in your heart and then let it go. If it stays allow it to stay. If it goes allow it to go. No thing is meant to remain, in both external and internal worlds.

Except you. The authentic you. The soundless, imageless, idealess you, who are, in essence, no one.

In the formal context of an organization there are two dimensions to leadership - strategy and character. As you can probably surmise this is a book about character and both the 'personal and people dimensions' of leadership.

It's about everyone's character as everyone is a potential leader in the context of their relationships, in both formal or informal settings.

If you would like to explore the other dimension of organizational leadership known as 'strategy', ask Professor Google to be your guide!

Frequently Asked Questions

1 If being no one is an actuality, who is it that is being no one?

There is no one there. When I say 'no one' I mean a being who has created an identity for itself. There is just being. Prior to the creation of any sense of 'I am Fred' or 'I am Mary', there is just a sense of 'I am'. But 'I am' is not even thought. There is just the awareness that I am.

If you master the art of meditation and you will realize and 'know' this for your self.

But of course, you cannot just be. You are animating and occupying a body, so you are here to act. You are acting in the material world in which we have created a physical language to name things and be able to physically communicate with each other, including the naming of the form you are in. In English, it was decided to call that form a 'body'!

The 'being' that we each are has been creating actions through form for some time. It's tiring, physically. So, the body requires sleep. Sleep is required for the body to rest and renew. Physical sleep also helps the mind think less as mental tiredness also affects the energy of the body.

It's also useful, some would say essential, to learn how to concentrate the mind when fully awake. That also reduces the quantity and speed of thought. In this age of superfast technologies, we tend to do too much thinking that is also too fast.

Mental tiredness seems more like a kind of confusion, a cloudiness within our awareness. We lose our ability to focus our thoughts and direct our attention. And when we are physically tired the primary 'instrument' of consciousness, which is the brain, also becomes tired and we experience brain fog. Rest the brain with a good night's sleep and it works better next morning. Rest the mind by learning to meditate and it then works better. Eventually!

The inner desktop

Imagine you've been working all day gradually building many files on your computer. Each file is something else you've been thinking about. By the end of the day your desktop screen is filled with file names. You've got some time left in the day, now which file do you go to? Which one gets your attention?

OK so you choose, but in the background there are quick fire thoughts breaking through saying, "I should also finish that one", or "This one over there needs more attention etc." You are not your mind and you are not the files, but they are shouting for your attention. You are that attention. When you go to sleep it's as if all the files are forgotten and the icons on your inner screen, so to speak, just melt into the background. Rest at last. When you wake up the next day your inner screen (your mind) is clear and you start filling it again. Sometimes superfast.

That's a simple way to explain why we become mentally tired. Every relationship, task or process has its own file within your consciousness. The file name and icon shows up on the screen of your mind. Not your brain. Your mind.

But the energy of being, of you, often referred to as spirit or spiritual energy, doesn't run down like the physical energy of the body. It fills up with mental business. It also starts to become sleepy, which means you lose the sharpness and freshness of awareness and attention.

Up until a certain point awareness is fresh and clear, to the degree that you remain free, unattached and unidentified with anything physical or mental. But slowly, and you can watch this happening to your self, you lose the sharpness of awareness to the degree that some images appearing on the screen of your mind become very inviting. They 'attract' your attention. Remember 'attention' is you. They attract you.

The most powerful image on the screen of your mind is the image of your body as you look down or look in a mirror. You create the image of your body on the screen of your mind. While it seems to be 'out there' it is really 'in here', on your mind. Slowly but surely your spiritual sleepiness i.e. the gradual diminishing of awareness, allows an illusion to occur, the illusion that 'I am this form' and that is all I am.

As soon as that part of the slippery slope kicks in it's not long before all the other 'mental images' connected to the body in the material world become attractive. We then start to identify with them. Clothes, dwellings, cars, places, the forms of other embodied beings etc.

In parallel, as we lose our freshness of being, as we lose our clarity of awareness, our natural quiet contentment, our enthusiastic joyfulness, our loving kindness, all diminish within our consciousness. Suddenly sensual, physical stimulation feels good. Eventually it seems to be the only way to feel OK. That's when physical sensual pleasure replaces the natural happiness of consciousness.

Suddenly pleasure, which is derived through sensual stimulation, from outside in, becomes addictive. Then one day we are so fast asleep i.e. unaware, we believe the physical material world is our primary reality, the only reality. We believe that our happiness lies somewhere 'out there' in the sensual world.

But all the while, deep down, prior to all those layers of memorized, material images and experiences, your original and natural state of being remains. A state of being where it was 'unnecessary' to create a sense of who I am, a self-identity, based on, well, anything. A state of being from which arose a natural contentedness, a natural peacefulness, a natural lovefulness.

This, in essence, is how we all 'fall' from 'being' consciousness to 'form' consciousness. On the way there, as well as on arrival, there is what we call suffering. It's the price we pay for falling asleep at the wheel of our life. It happens to us all. At least I have not yet encountered anyone to whom this has not happened.

But it's OK. It's what is meant to happen. You can't wake up unless you've fallen asleep. You cannot consciously know and appreciate the waking state unless there is a period of sleep. You cannot realize and fully appreciate your self-responsibility and your creative capacity until you lose it!

2 Is anyone ever someone?

Today almost everyone is under the illusion they are someone. Just looking in a mirror is enough to trigger the programmed belief 'that's me'. Or they aspire to be somebody who is recognized by others in the world as 'somebody special'. The classic symptom is the pursuit of fame at some level or other. Not only have we learned to believe we are just material beings but we create the desire for the recognition of other material beings. We make our self-esteem and self-worth dependent on our physical appearance and our physical actions being esteemed by others. Then we believe this dependency is natural. But it's a dependency. And all dependency is unnatural. Agree? Mmm!

In reality, everyone is, in essence, no one. Realize that and you will start to see (be aware of) your self and others, in an entirely different light. You will start to understand why people do what they do, feel what they feel and believe what they believe.

3 What's the point of life and living if you and I, and everyone else, is no one?

We cannot stay static in that silent and still state of being and also know the fullness of living and the expression (pressing out) of our creative power. In that state we cannot know the beauty of our being and that of others. Just as a seed cannot remain a seed if it is to create its own form, fragrance and color. Life and living the journey through matter, time and space, gives us the opportunity to bring the best of our self into expression and therefore into the world.

Like any journey the terrain you pass through rises and falls. Why do we like to travel? Because we enjoy experiencing the rising and falling of the terrain. We enjoy experiencing the different vistas on the way. If it was all mountains or all desert or all ocean we'd become bored and take everything for granted. If our inner life was all peace and beauty, all harmony and lightness, we'd likely become bored and take everything for granted.

'Life as a journey' is a well-used metaphor for our spiritual journey, for the journey of consciousness into matter, then to create thoughts and actions and express them through matter in the material world. You get the opportunity to create and experience all possible experiences. You travel through some terrible terrain i.e. you create dark feelings due to ignorance as a result of becoming sleepy i.e. the loss of the awareness that you are just 'being'. But mostly the journey is a magnificent voyage filled with many experiences and insperiences of great beauty.

But just as on any physical journey tiredness is inevitable. On our spiritual journey, the journey of consciousness into matter and subsequent creative process, we become sleepy as our awareness dulls. Our character slowly diminishes and the quality of our creation slowly deteriorates. The main sign is an increase in suffering. Not pain, but suffering. But you also get to find your way back, rediscover and recover your self, and thereby consciously spiritualize your creation and liberate your self from suffering.

The end result is a return to your natural state. You actually become consciously aware you are no one. At the very beginning of the journey you were also no one, but you were not aware that you were no one. In the first instance, at the beginning of the journey, it's called 'pure innocence'. But we didn't name it like that, describe it like that, we just were it! Like a baby is 'innocent' when it's born. It doesn't know it, it just is it. In the second instance, which is now, you can consciously realize you are no one. It's called the 'wisdom of being innocent'. Now we are aware of it and now we name it, describe it.

And when you 'know' it then whatever you create is shaped and influenced by it.

Well that's how I might describe journey in a couple of paragraphs! You can use different words and perhaps a lot more words.

Understanding this fall from being no one to believing you are someone, and all the illusions and experiences along the way, allows you to cultivate a wisdom that you then bring to the way you relate and interact with others today.

You now know that all your unhappiness, stress, suffering has its roots in one mistake i.e. that I believe I am somebody. Which leads to other mistakes such as I am handsome or ugly, I am this fashion-wear, I am these things which represent my material success, I am my occupation, I am the lover of this person etc. etc. No, you're not. You, the authentic you, are none of those things. That may seem obvious, but if you become upset when anything happens to any of those 'things' or they don't do what you want, it means your identity, your sense of who you are, is invested in them. That's the mistake.

When you 'know' you are no one then you no longer need to be seen as 'someone' by others. Paradoxically others will recognize you even more but in a different way. Why, because your energy, your attitude, is different. It's not that when being no one means you do nothing. The purpose of living is to 'create doing', to create actions! For your self as well as for and with others.

We occupy and animate a physical form. It's that material form that gives us the opportunity to create a life. The form we occupy is also something we need to look after, take care of, maintain. Unfortunately, we are not aware that we are not 'it'. We believe we are form and we believe that's all we are. So most of us abuse it.

We eat too much, we become vain, we over use it by working too much etc. It's the belief that we are only a material form that leads to the illusion that physical pleasure equals the only happiness. So instead of taking care of it we use it to indulge our self with feelings of pleasure which we collectively mistake for happiness. (but don't tell Hollywood!). That's why we face universal issues such as obesity, diabetes, addiction etc. in almost every society, regardless of the culture of that society.

As co-creators, we also get to see our self in human terms in the mirror of our relationships. We get to show others our humanity and mirror their humanity. This is the essence of leadership, showing your own humanity and facilitating others 'humanity'.

But first, it's necessary to discover your own authenticity for your self and then be that 'authenticity' for others. And that's just not possible until you realize that, in essence, you are no one. It's becoming increasingly obvious that the world is now waiting for this level of leadership.

4 How on earth do I operate in the world while being no one?

OK, let's assume you've restored and mastered the consciousness of being no one. It's not that you are no longer here or not capable or you just don't do anything. Now you play the game of life without the constraints of the fear of what others think of you, without the fear of losing something which you never possessed in the first place, without the fear of missing out on anything and without the fear of being criticized.

You, the being that is no one, are in and animating a material form. You get to be an independent being in control of your body. Like a driver in control of their car. You get to create a life in the material context of the world through your body. And you get the opportunity to do that with other embodied beings.

You get to create and play as many roles as you would like. And in the creating and playing those roles you get to choose your experiences and 'insperiences'. How well you play your role/s is up to you. It will depend on how natural you are, on how close you are to your natural and true state of being. The closer you are the more authentic you will appear to others, the more they will connect and want to connect with you. When you create and play your roles in life 'from' that sense of authenticity, you are not thinking, "Aha now I am playing this role or that role". You are simply creating and playing what is appropriate in that moment. When what you do create is appropriate and accurately aligned and arising out of your authenticity, there arises feelings of satisfaction, meaningfulness and fulfillment. They emerge naturally from inside out.

But your ability to create and play your roles with authenticity is sabotaged by your beliefs and ideas about your self, about *who* you believe you should be, and *how* you should be, about *what* you want and believe you 'should get' from others in terms of recognition and respect. It's these beliefs that are in the way and stopping you being authentic and therefore allowing your authentic character to emerge. Especially the belief that you are either someone special or that you should be trying to be someone special.

So, the paradoxical essence is, if you want to create and play your role of manager, brother, friend, parent, leader etc. brilliantly well, then don't 'identify' with the role. You and I are not roles. Just as the actor is not the role. But we get to create and play as many roles as we want.

Improvise well

Have you ever seen actors improvising? They have no idea what will happen once they are on the stage. They improvise their roles as the scene develops. They create it there and then. No rehearsal, no script, no preconceived ideas. They don't 'think' about it.

Life is a bit like that in its raw essence. You can decide who or what you will create and play. You can decide what role is necessary for the scene you are in. But here's the rub. The more you think about it the less real and original, and the less creative, you will likely be. The more you think about it the less easily it will flow and gel with those who are in the same scene with you. When you pre-determine how you will play a role before you are 'in the scene' you automatically create an agenda in your relationships with others. Having an agenda, which is code for wanting certain results/outcomes, in any relationship, ensures you will think too much, compromise your character, thereby sabotaging your creative spontaneity, thereby ensuring the diminishment of any feelings of meaningfulness and fulfillment. After a while it becomes tiring and depleting. That's often when that question jumps into your head as it punctures any remaining enthusiasm with, "What's the point?"

Pure creativity does not come from thinking, it arises from a free and open state of being. In other words, only when there is nothing in the way. What we put 'in the way' are thoughts like, "Mmm, I think I should be more like this" or, "Should I say this or that" or "I hope they will like my way of doing it". Or memories like, " I hope they're not going to be in the same mood as last time".

You won't be able to create with ease if you are trying to live up to what you imagine other's perceptions of you are. You can't be spontaneously creative if you want people to see you a certain way (unless you are a comedian!! but even that cannot be maintained). You won't be naturally creative if you believe someone is about to take away what you believe is yours or simply steal the scene.

You cannot create authentically and know the joy that comes with that creativity until you realize you are no one. Until you have no thought for what others think about you, no thought for the protection of your reputation, no thought about needing to make an impression or for the maintenance of your position in the set of relationships in which you are acting.

Although you could say we are all actors, that we are creators of the actions that make up our role in any given scene, there is a crucial difference between you and an actor on a theatre stage. Before actors start to play a part in a movie or on stage they read the script, rehearse the part and 'get into' character. In order to play the game of life and 'enjoy', (which means 'be in joy') the many scenes that you will find your self in, it's necessary to allow your character to 'flow out' of you unscripted, in its free and liberated form. It cannot be shaped by a script. It is not pre-scribed. It cannot be manufactured to any particular specification ...and remain authentic.

Searching for home

In the process of forgetting that we are no one or trying to be someone, our natural character has been forgotten or blocked and distorted on its way from inside out. That temporary loss of so many of the natural traits that make up our character (see profile), and the resultant suffering, has made us search for what we feel has been lost.

Not having found our natural, authentic self/character we settled for the next best thing i.e. we learned to believe that we need to 'learn' how to be good, learn how to be caring, learn how to love, learn how to be open, learn how to be witty, how to be endearing, how to be charismatic etc. etc.

Enter the learning and development industry and suddenly we 'believe' such traits can be learned, should be learned, need to be learned. Before we know it, we are paying a lot of money to learn how to 'be and do' what is already intrinsic to our character.

say your boss wants you to be a leader for the team. So, you play the role of leader. Break it down and that might sometimes include the roles of facilitator or coordinator or fellow worker or team captain or motivator or mediator etc. But what kind of character is required for all of those roles. Open, caring, empathic, encouraging, honest, accepting, appreciative etc., but at different unpredictable moments in different unpredictable ways in different unpredictable scenes and situations. Such attributes are innate to our character when we are being our authentic self. But they only emerge in the accurate way in the relevant scene when there is nothing in way such as inhibiting thoughts, "I need to be seen to be efficient or effective or successful or brilliant or competent".

Yes, different traits for different moments, but they are all relevant regardless of the roles we play. But if we build our sense of who I am from an idea or concept of the role, then such traits will not emerge easily or accurately. As witnessed every day in almost every workplace.

Paradoxically, being no one, which means being totally free on the inside, free of trying to be the ideal, makes your energy, your character, attractive to others (but don't tell them you are no one!!). As a consequence, into your life will come more opportunities as well as greater challenges to test you, to experiment with, to be creative, to be co-creative etc.

Being no one is the ultimate humility. Demonstrated in such moments when things don't go to plan and yet you are seen and felt to remain calm, focused and creatively proactive. You will not be able to be seen like that if you have identified your self with a desired outcome or that you were in possession of something that has been damaged or lost. You will be panicky, upset and worried.

No, being no one doesn't make you look weak or like someone who doesn't care!! Your care is real and now much more expansive to include others and what they are going through, compared to what it was i.e. narrowly focused on your self, how you were feeling, and worried what others might be thinking about you.

5 What do you mean exactly by self-lessness?

Imagine you are in a car and it's being driven by remote control by someone outside. You have no choice, but to go where it takes you, where they direct it to go. You do not have the power to control your direction or to choose your destination. You become frustrated that while you are trapped in the car someone else is making it go in a direction you would not choose.

This is a metaphor for most people's lives today. They are being driven by remote control, otherwise known as the subconscious. That's why we become reactive, why we create emotional reactions, why we say and do things we often regret later. It's why we don't feel free and in control of our life.

It's the 'recordings' of beliefs and emotions, thinking patterns and reactions, within our subconscious, that are controlling our life. The deepest recordings are those that contain 'who I believe I am' and 'what I believe is mine'. Only when those beliefs are sourced, challenged and realized to be 'not true', can you free your self from the remote control, so to speak. Only then can your personal destiny be returned fully, consciously, back to your hands. Otherwise your consciousness and all its functions are being run by recordings, often termed conditioning, which has a false sense of self behind everything you create.

This is one meaning of being self-less whereby all the false identities the self has created and recorded are now gone. The other meaning is when you are being unselfish. True self-lessness is when you act and respond with no thought of 'what's in it for me'. That's only truly possible when you've realized nothing 'real' can ever be acquired and kept. To an enlightened soul things and positions, and even other people, are always changing, coming and going, therefore not real. Reality in this context is that which never changes. That's the real, authentic you. Yes, other people have a 'real them' that never changes too.

But here in this material world they also come and go and ...change! Selflessness means you meet and accept them as they are, which means in whatever state of consciousness you find them. But you don't try to change them, hang on to them or make them 'mine' or become dependent on them or use them to affirm your own sense of who you are.

6 How long does it take to become 'no one' and move through life with consummate ease?

Well if you ask 'how long' will it take, it's already taking too long! It's not a question of time, more a question of interest. How interested are you and how sustained will your interest be? It's different for different people. There may be moments of tremendous insight and realization. There will also be times when nothing seems to be shifting, when no new insights are occurring. But as long as you are interested and therefore integrating some of the practices (see The Practices) into your life then there will be movement. How do you know? Well you'll become calmer and more open to others. Your difficult relationships will become easier. Life in general will be more fulfilling and meaningful. Things will happen with a greater sense of ease.

Yet there will be times, periods or phases, when none of that happens, perhaps even the opposite. Everyone is different and awakens differently.

7 But don't we need a worldly identity to negotiate and navigate our way through what is a worldly life?

Yes we all do. But the key is to see such 'worldly identities' as roles that you play. Make life play full! But don't forget, YOU are not the role. You are not the necessary worldly identity. When you go through passport control you act and answer as if you are the nationality stated on your passport. But within your consciousness you know that you are not a nationality.

Nationality is just another idea and you are not an idea. So when someone criticizes the nationality which you have been given, it doesn't bother you, you don't take personally, so you don't create emotional suffering for your self. You certainly don't start a fight!

Now expand that out into all the other ideas you have been taught to identify with including race, religion, culture, gender etc. and suddenly you begin to see you are the one who adopts the idea, plays with the idea, speaks the language of those ideas, but you are not the idea. Just as you put clothes on your body every day you know the clothes are not your body, but you still wear them.

Worldly identities are like clothing for consciousness. You put them on, engage with the world, then take them off. When you can do this and be aware you are doing this, allowing your spontaneity to shine through, then you'll notice how you've become the master of your consciousness again. No longer do the recordings take over, no longer does the programming/conditioning take over. You are free on the inside and you notice how one sign of that freedom is the gradual reduction and ultimate ending of suffering and indeed the cessation of any remaining vestiges of unhappiness.

8 What does being no one and having nothing really got to do with leadership – surely there is a contradiction?

Every leader is first and foremost a human being. Every human is a potential leader by example. Every human being is conscious and therefore consciousness. We have all learned to make same mistakes within consciousness, within our self. Hence the necessity to correct those mistakes at the level of our consciousness 'in here' if we are to be an effective leader, in any context, 'out there'.

Each of us can only build and sustain our relationships with others according to the capacity and authenticity of our character. Restoring our authenticity is no small task. It has to start back on the drawing board, so to speak, with who and what I am. If the awareness of who and what I am is not clear, and it isn't, simply because we have all learned to make the same mistakes, then everything that arises out of that will not be accurate, it will not be authentic.

So it's not a contradiction, it's more like relaying the very foundations of our life and the way in which we will live from inside out. Right now most of us are living from outside in and that's a fundamental mistake which diminishes our capacity to lead others and be an example for others.

HAVING NOTHING

... and the Art of Being Free

"Have you ever noticed how every 'thing' and everyone comes and goes? No thing stays forever. No one stays forever. Coming and going are the primary and most natural patterns of change in our busy world."

Having nothing does not mean you get up one morning and give the keys to your house and car away. It just means you change your relationship in your mind with such 'things', so that you can enjoy them, without craving them, while they are there, and when they go, as they must, it's OK. Having nothing does not mean you give all your money to charity and take a vow of poverty. It just means you use the money that flows into and out of your life with wisdom and care. Having nothing does not mean you disown family or friends, husbands or wives. It just means you cease to be attached to them in a way that allows you to be more consistently and lovingly open, honest and accepting of them. Having nothing does not mean you have no 'stuff' in your life. It just means the 'stuff' doesn't have you!

When you have a relationship of attachment to things, people, positions and reputations, it means you are creating the illusion of possession. Then you use the illusion of possession to create an illusion of who you are as you use what you believe you have, to build your sense of self!

It doesn't matter how intelligent or enlightened you may consider your self to be, if you still believe you possess ...anything, it will kill your joy. Temporary pleasure is possible, but the internal joy of a constant and underlying dancing of your heart, is not possible. Pleasure cannot replace happiness. But it's in the trying that addiction and dependency arise.

Whenever we use the word 'my', either in thought or speech, we are affirming the illusion 'that is mine', as in my house, my car, my neighborhood, my ideas, my beliefs, my nation, my party etc. Then we use the 'they are mine' idea, when we refer to the people in our life, as in my family, my friends, my boss, my company, my 'other half' etc.

OK, so we know they are not mine, as in 'belong' to me. We know we do not possess other people or abstract ideas like nations and philosophies etc. But then we act and react as if we do.

An inside job

This idea that 'they' and 'that' are mine, and therefore 'belong' to me, is the sign you have created an attachment to 'them' within your consciousness. That's where attachment happens. This attachment, any attachment, means you are not free. You become trapped in your attachment in your own mind for a few seconds here, a few minutes there or perhaps many years with your deepest attachments. Perhaps a lifetime!

This is where all fear comes from. Any attachment to anything means fear in the form of anxiety, insecurity, tension, worry, panic etc., is inevitable. Which then skews your 'decision making' capabilities, sabotaging your openness and honesty, while diminishing your ability to build trusting and empathic relationships.

It's really that simple. It's also another reason why we cannot 'learn' how to 'do' openness, honesty, empathy, compassion etc. The anxiety, insecurity, tension and worry habits will always get in the way. Until there is the realization that, in reality, we have nothing, it's almost impossible to free our self from such emotional habits!

It's not a pretty picture as most relationships are based on attachment and therefore tend to be infected by such fears. Fear of loss, fear of damage, fear of rejection, fear of insult, fear of being overwhelmed, fear of unmet expectations, fear of being disrespected.

We are often good at disguising our fears. If you are in a position of any responsibility you will likely try to hide your emotion/s, which means suppress your fear. And that's what we generally learn to do while becoming quite adept at doing so. The behaviors that are then shaped by that hiding and suppression are not ones of an authentic character and therefore not of someone who will lead others ...well!

This makes it sound as if attachment, possession, fear, are wrong and bad. But they're not. They occur. They are developed. They are habits that are recreated and expressed by millions of people every day in a thousand ways. Unfortunately our societies, our cultures, have become dependent on us 'believing in possession' i.e. that we can possess something, that attachment is perfectly natural, that our possessions are a source of the pleasures that we mistake for happiness. We are even prepared to pay the price of attachment, of holding the illusion of possession, which is some amount of fear in its daily stressful forms of insecurity and anxiety.

Most industries in the world are totally dependent on our belief in possessing. They rely on our habit of becoming attached to objects, people and places and our consequent fearfulness.

a) It allows them to convince us we need the latest model/fashion/vacation etc., in order to relieve our emotional suffering and be happy...again!

b) It encourages them to highlight and scare us with a 'problem', which, if we do not fix it will lead to some form of loss. (all fear is the fear of loss). Then of course they present us with the solution and therefore the promise to alleviate and eliminate our fear.

Once again, it's not wrong or bad. It's just a trap we have all fallen for. They know not what they do! It's just an inaccurate way to understand our relationship with things and people. Most especially that thing called money.

While most of us understand and admit that we cannot buy or acquire happiness, we live and purchase things as if we can. We are trapped in the belief that 'having' something or someone is the only way to live the good and happy life.

Liberation from such a belief requires the realization that it's an illusion while accepting complete responsibility for both the feelings and the actions that we create. That's usually only possible when we experience the feelings of meaningfulness and fulfillment that we generate for our self when we start 'giving selflessly' to others.

Not only does it become obvious that you cannot possess anything, you cease to believe that you need to. This level of liberation from illusion then allows you to perceive and relate to people and things in an 'accurate' way. You recognize every 'thing' comes into your life for use. Everything has a purpose. But its purpose is not to be used to define your 'self' or even 'make' you happy. Every person that comes into your life arrives so you can:

a) co-create something together

b) they come to teach you, show you, make you aware, of something you did not know, usually about yourself.

Often, it's both.

The result of realizing nothing is mine is you no longer generate fear of loss. You cannot lose what you do not have. The restoration of this 'right relationship' with things and people liberates the self from the habits of creating fear and sadness in all their forms. This is the real meaning of freedom.

You no longer paralyze or distort your own character. You cease to see others or situations as a threat. Your position at work can be threatened, but you cannot. You are not your position. Your job can be threatened. But you cannot. You are not your job, you are not what you do. You do not possess the position or the job. You are free. If your position or job is taken away, as everything is, eventually, it's not a problem. It just means you have some new choices to make, that's all!

Even if your partner leaves you, you are not losing them. They don't 'belong' to you. They have just decided to travel in a different direction. Once again you have some new choices to make. But if you make your self sad and angry in any way, it just means you are holding that person in your consciousness as a personal possession. You are demonstrating your dependency and therefore you are not the master of your own life.

Sounds a bit harsh, doesn't it? But it's necessarily so, if we are going to break out of the illusion of possession, of believing we 'have' something or someone.

As a result of shattering the illusion of possession the characteristics that then emerge naturally, from within you, include an ease with others that allows you to stay open, curious, transparent and giving. As you no longer hide and hold on to what is not yours, most of your anxieties disappear. Nothing can ever be lost! Get it!

The Example You Are!

If we are living in constant anxiety/worry at possible loss we will not be able to bring empathy, respect, openness and honesty to the table of relationship. There will always be someone who says or does something that we perceive to be a threat to what we believe is 'mine'. Simply arguing with someone drains our energy and self-inflicts suffering called frustration and fear. It's caused by holding on to the illusion of 'my opinion'. Which really means the illusion that 'my' belief is true and it's mine. Which is another way of saying, "This is the only valid point of view forever and it belongs to me, me, me".

Have you ever met someone who responds differently by saying things like, "That's an interesting viewpoint", or "I'm curious to understand why you think that," or "How do you see it that way", or "Tell me more", or "Do you think that's the most accurate way to assess the situation"?

Who would you rather hang out with? Who would you 'follow' into a conversation? If you were invited onto a debating team who would you rather have on your side? The opinionated arguer, always projecting and defending 'my' beliefs? Or the open and curious dialoguer, always curious and interested to see and understand the depth of everything.

In any conversation, the one who asks the questions, not the one who apparently has all the answers, is the leader of the conversation! But we won't ask questions, we won't be curious to understand, if we are holding on to a position, an opinion, which we then fear being wrong, which is code for 'lost'.

Frequently Asked Questions

1 How do I have nothing while everything remains?

The illusion of 'possessing' originates within our consciousness not within our hands. It's the relationship that we have with things, people and ideas 'within our self', that constitutes our belief in possession or not.

It's the closing of our 'self' around the idea or the image of what we learn to believe is 'mine'. Usually accompanied by the belief that the object or person satisfies us, fulfills us, completes us, makes us happy! All illusions, unfortunately. When you increase your self-awareness you'll see exactly how you lose your self 'in' such images and ideas within your own mind.

That's why it's useful to sit quietly and watch your self. Watch how you habitually use what you believe is 'mine' to construct your sense of self. Then, how the thoughts that emerge in your mind about what you believe is 'me and mine' are shaped by that image or idea. Then, notice how you sometimes misuse your imagination (imaging capacity) and you imagine 'it' or 'they' will be gone. How you then create sadness, anger or fear. Possibly all three. And that is what suffering is, that's why and how it's created.

2 'Where' do you have nothing?

In your consciousness. But only when you are being your self, which is consciousness itself. When you no longer attach your self to what is on your mind then 'you' are free. Mind is a faculty of consciousness that you use to create ideas and images of things and people and places. It's where you give form to your thoughts. Where you run stories like a movie on the screen. But the mistake we make is the 'I' that says 'I am' goes into the images and ideas, gets lost in the images and ideas, then uses the images and ideas to build a sense of 'who I am'. Not recommended, but probably the one habit we are all schooled in from the day we arrive.

It doesn't mean you give everything and everyone that is in your life today away! You still use objects and build relationships with people. But you change your relationship to objects and people to one of non-attachment. You do that within your consciousness, within you, by not attaching your self to what is on your mind.

3 Does anyone ever have or possess anything or anyone?

No. It's impossible for consciousness, which is what you/I/we are to possess anything or anyone. But please don't believe me! See for your self.

4 What's the point of living if you have nothing?

The point of living is not to acquire and possess. It's to give of your best. You cannot do that if you have possessions which you believe are mine. The fear and sadness, anger and anxiety, that is generated as a result of the illusion of possession sabotages your ability to be and give of the best of you, the highest, of you. People and things are in your life but they are not 'mine'! They do not give you happiness. Happiness is what you are, but only when there is no longer any attachment.

People don't give you the love that you seek. Love is what you are. But only when you are non-dependent, which is the same as non-attached. Once you realize this it becomes obvious that the point of your life is to give of your best, which is the way to create your life. That's why we are here. Not to 'get a life' but to create our life. That depends on the quality of your consciousness which, in turn, depends on how free you are within your self.

5 What's wrong with wanting more for me?

It's called greed, as we all now know. It's also a sign of dependency and addiction. It's one of the oldest ways known to man and woman to pursue the illusion of happiness and thereby create unhappiness. It's selfish and thereby creates division and conflict. Watch the news, read a paper, take in a movie. Almost every message you allow into your consciousness from the world 'out there' is about some form of greed.

The language is, "I want". The illusion is, "When I get what I want I'll be happy". The outcome is, "I am not happy". If you pursue happiness 'out there' in the world you are guaranteed to make your self unhappy!

It's not about wrong or right, it's just a habitual mistake that a sleepy consciousness falls into. We all need to correct the same mistakes, including me, if we want to liberate our self from suffering, stress, sorrow, be truly free on the inside and thereby allow our authentic character to re-emerge from inside out.

6 You said having nothing brings you everything, what do you mean?

Yes it's a paradox to an unenlightened mind. When you realize you have nothing, that nothing and no one can be possessed by you, it means everything and everyone becomes available to you. When you are no longer busy wrapping your self, your consciousness, around what you believe is mine, when you stop holding on, or adding to your illusory stash of possessions, it means your perception, your awareness, opens like a flower and suddenly you are available to everyone else and they are available to you.

This can be an ever-expanding awareness/perception if you would like it to be. In essence, the more you realize you have nothing the more of everything is available for you. Experiment. See for your self. It's not a big deal. Just a reality that has been ignored and forgotten in favor of the illusion and the false promise of acquiring happiness by acquiring things.

7 Is there not a feeling of emptiness when you have nothing and no one, a feeling of isolation and loneliness?

It may seem that that is what will happen. But that's because you imagine what it might be like, instead of going there to see for your self. It's like imagining a country is a dark and horrible place because that is what you have learned to imagine, it's an image you have developed in your imagination. But then, one day, you go there and discover it's a delightfully sunny place with delightfully sunny people. You wonder why or how you could have imagined it otherwise.

It's also a bit like telling a drug addict you have taken away their drugs and they cannot have anymore. Choose your metaphor!

It's challenging your attachment and dependency on what and who you have grown up to believe are mine. But if you want to taste and understand what real freedom feels like, it's necessary to go and see and feel for your self, in your own way, in your own time.

Then you will likely discover that yes, you may be totally alone, but you are never lonely! But that's another seminar!

8 With so many references to suffering and what is unnaturally created in consciousness such as sadness, anger and fear, what then remains if we do free our self from such emotions?

When there is an end to the creation of what is unnatural, what is left is 'the natural' or your true nature. No more emotions but a multitude of feelings that you could not consistently insperience before. Love suddenly has many ways to be expressed and therefore felt. Not romantic or desirous love, but the 'self as love', expressed as acceptance, care and openness towards others. A contentment with everyone and everything that is occurring around you, close and far. A quiet joy in the simple acts of living. A sense of the beauty which you were not able to perceive when you were anxious or sad. An equal appreciation for both the small and big things that enter your life. A deep sense of significance and meaningfulness behind everything you do arises, naturally. The paradox of fulfilment ceases to be a paradox. In other words, you realize you 'feel full filled' in life when you give of your self unconditionally, in lively ways. Essentially, what is true and natural is allowed to flourish when what is unnatural is no more. Between there and here, there may be a small matter of an addiction to fear, and addiction to angriness and an addiction to sorrow. In other words, an addiction to suffering. Hence the necessity of 'the practices', which we explore later.

By the way...

Perhaps the most common belief, that so many of us seem to carry, is that a little sadness, a little fear and a little anger, are perfectly natural. And that it's also OK if we move from a little to a lot! It is, they say, 'human nature' to feel these emotions, to be stressed out, to feel the emotional heat!! It's just part of life's rich pageant ...they say!

But when you notice that the cause of all your stress can be attributed to our three radical insights you will also notice that such beliefs stand in the way, within our consciousness, of ever discovering your authenticity and bringing the highest attributes of your character to your relationships.

No one makes you sad or happy, fearful or loving, angry or serene. We do that. You do that. I do that. To our self. We are each responsible. If that penny doesn't drop it's hard to make both the external and internal journeys.

Calling such emotions 'natural' then becomes an excuse to do nothing. We not only believe others are responsible for any and all our unhappiness, but we also make our self a victim of our own creation, which we then conveniently believe we can do nothing about.

So, we learn to believe it's natural to suffer and it's natural to be a victim! And that it's therefore natural to be helpless, unable to change what and how we feel.

It's no wonder the world becomes stranger by the day as we accentuate and magnify such beliefs and project them onto more people and into more contexts.

It's not that sadness, anger and fear are bad! They are not bad, as in the opposite of good, they are just mistakes, miscreations, due to assimilating and, albeit subconsciously, holding on to inaccurate beliefs.

GOING NOWHERE

...and the Art of Presence

*"Have you ever noticed how the anticipation
is often greater than the realization. You
imagine how great the holiday is going
to be but when you get there you are
still in your miserable mindset.
That's why 'wherever you
go there you are'!"*

Realizing you are going nowhere does not mean you stay in bed all day.   But you do set your self free of the habit of creating the feeling, sometimes a 'pressure feeling', that you need to be somewhere other than where you are.   Going nowhere does not mean you are stuck, useless and without the capacity to achieve anything. It means you've realized that your ambitiousness to get on and be somewhere significant in the eyes of others has been exposed as an illusory aspiration that can never fulfill you. Going nowhere does not mean you don't go to where the sun beckons and the azure sea, surrounded by lush green mountains, are awaiting to embrace you. It just means that some geographical locations in the world have more sunshine for your body, but not for 'you', to soak up! Going nowhere does not mean you have no future. It just means you live in the present and, as you do, you become more present *with* others and therefore a powerful presence *for* others.   Which, paradoxically, ensures you will have a prosperous future!

It's not that you don't travel or you don't take your body to other places. You do, but you also know that wherever in the world you travel the real journey is internal not external. Which means wherever your body goes so you, with all your worries and anxieties, are still 'here'. Not 'here' as in an external physical location, but 'here' as in within your consciousness, which is your self.

While you may alter the 'state' in a country in which you locate your body, your state of being stays the same. While you may change the physical location of your body you do not change the location of ...you. Well, you do, actually! You leave your center and go into your mind and try to live in a jungle of ever changing thoughts. You exit your throne at the heart of your being and go live in your habits. You swing like Tarzan through the jungle of your memories, the jungle of your self-created habitual beliefs, emotions and attitudes. Thoughts and habits are 'places' in the universe of consciousness. But they are subtle places, you could call them subtle things, in the inner space of you.

But we are mostly unaware this takes place. We have learned to believe we are just another body so we fall under the illusion that wherever our body goes we go too. You do, but you don't! Not an easy illusion to expose. It requires a level of introspection and awareness that eventually leads to the realization that the 'I' that says 'I am' occupies and animates form, but is not to be confused with form.

That you are the non-material entity known as consciousness cannot be proven scientifically. But you can prove it to yourself through the practice of meditation. It's in meditation that you transcend the consciousness of the body or what is sometimes referred to as 'body consciousness'.

You insperience and know your 'self' to be beyond the limitations of the material world 'out there'. But you also realize you have been mistaking your self for your body for a long time. So, when the form that you occupy goes 'somewhere' in the physical world you have mistakenly learned to believe that you do to. And you do, but only in the material context of the outer world. But you don't go anywhere in the context of your consciousness, the inner world of being. There, you are always 'here'!

When you restore the awareness of being consciousness itself, the primary environment for you, the conscious being, ceases to be the room, the garden, the office, the home. The primary context is not a landscape but more like a 'beingscape' that includes the mind and its ability to give invisible form to invisible thought. It includes the intellect which makes invisible evaluations and invisible decisions. And 'in there', which is in you, is also memory, where you record all that is invisible and internally created by you within consciousness, within you. This is the context that is within you, regardless of wherever you go 'out there'!

It's into memory that we tend to try to escape the present moment. Hence the material success of the nostalgia industries. It's in memory that we become absent from the present. Even when we are listening to someone 'out there' we go into memory 'in here'. What they say triggers memories which generate thoughts in our mind. Those thoughts form a story, so we create a story and then watch the story unfold within our mind. Which then shapes the personal meaning we create. Unless we are vigilant we will use those memories, which are essentially made of beliefs, to misjudge the other.

In memory, we escape to what seemed like a better past. A time and period that we deem was better than the present. Or we allow our self to be drawn back into thoughts and images of unfinished business. If there is any animosity or resentment in our memories that's a sure sign of unfinished business. Sometimes it's called 'your karma'

Even when we are future focused we are still using memories to create our speculative futures. Once again all of this is not wrong or bad. Just habits we all develop. But it's such habits that ensure we are not fully present, which then gets in the way of being a 'leading presence' in the lives of others.

Our effectiveness at influencing and leading others out of this jungle within, will be dependent to what extent we have exposed and dissolved our own illusions and freed our self from our own habits of drifting and swinging through our own inner jungle.

This is one of the reasons why mindfulness has enjoyed such a renaissance in the last ten years. The essence of any mindful practice is restoring 'present moment awareness'. It's the strengthening of our ability to not succumb to the temptation to go somewhere in the past or somewhere in the future, as we use memories to create 'thought stories' in our mind.

This 'drifting' habit, not helped by social media, interferes with our ability to concentrate on what we are doing. It breaks our connection and communication with others. And it drains our mental energy.

Mindfulness is a practice in which you train your self out of such habits and restore your ability to be fully aware of being here and now. When you do, you realize for your self that 'you' have never been anywhere nor are you ever going anywhere! You are always 'here'. That does not mean you physically sit in a chair for the rest of your days and do nothing. Of course, your body goes places. It travels. Perhaps a lot. But YOU don't. Get it?

When our favorite habits are to drift into speculative futures or back to nostalgic pasts, entirely within our consciousness, the content of each then tends to fill our conversations with regrets and hopes. This only adds to any feelings of helplessness based on the mistaken belief that we are not responsible for our life in this moment now.

Frequently Asked Questions

1 If I am going 'no where' why do I need a passport?

Very funny! You obviously need a passport if you physically travel to another country anywhere in the material world. It's a document that allows you to 'pass' through a 'port' which is a gateway to another 'state authority'. It's not a bad metaphor for what also needs to happen in consciousness.

You need to pass through an inner port that lies at the edge of your own authority. Right now, most of us try to live outside our own authority as we abdicate responsibility for what we feel and project it on to others. We then believe we are a victim of other's words or actions, or of events and circumstances. Your body may be a victim but 'the self' is not. But if you live in your habitual beliefs and emotions, if you live in your mind and in what's on your mind, you will conclude you are a victim.

The port we all need to pass though is called 'realization'. It's the realization that consciousness is what you are. You are stuck at border control until you realize this. You are being controlled by the illusion that you are somebody. Therefore, you believe you are being controlled by other embodied beings and the systems of approval, acceptance and acknowledgment they create. Only when you self-realize as the intangible energy of consciousness, can you once again become the authority of your being. Until then, all those habits, based on an inaccurate set of beliefs whereby you make your self unhappy, will have 'authority' over your 'state' of being. That means they have the authority to shape your thoughts, decisions, feelings and behaviors.

There is no science for this. There are no scientific studies or proofs. Science has nothing to say about consciousness. Simply because you cannot apply a scalpel to self or get consciousness into a test tube.

The 'effects' of consciousness can be scientifically observed as consciousness impacts the material object we call the brain. But the origin of such effects is in the invisible and intangible realm, and therefore in the non-observable world of consciousness. Correction! You can 'see' this for your self by cultivating your self-awareness. That's when you become both the scientist and the object of enquiry, subjectively speaking!

You cannot be an example of being your own authority to others, until you have exposed the illusions and delusions that arise from the mistake of believing the primary reality in life is the observable and measurable physical world.

2 Does this mean I have never been anywhere?

Yes. While your travels take you, within your body, to different locations in the material world you remain always 'here'. In the universe of consciousness, YOU only move into your mind and memories. In the universe of matter you change the physical location of the form you occupy many times a day.

In the universe of consciousness you move only into your thought 'forms', subtle feeling 'forms' and emotional 'forms'. While they are originated within your consciousness, within you, you learn to lose your self in such thought/feeling/emotional forms. And just like you learn to identify with your physical form so you also mistake your self for your thoughts and emotions. This is how the ego takes more subtle forms. How we give it life within consciousness.

Once again, it's not wrong or right. It's just a mistake we learn to make in our sleepiness, in our diminishing awareness. It's best not to start thinking thoughts like, "I should not think like this... I am bad because I keep making this mistake". That is not the way to liberation from illusion. Just the creation of more illusions.

3 Why bother living if we are all going nowhere?

Nothing says you should not explore the world, bring your joy to the world and thereby enjoy the world 'out there'. The mistake is just believing the world that seems to be 'out there' is all there is to enjoy. It's a limited world filled with finite things. Whereas your inner world, the universe of consciousness, is unlimited and infinite. When you practice any introspective methodology or technique you will start to become aware of this. Eventually you go beyond method and technique and you simply cultivate an ever deepening and broadening awareness of your own unlimitedness. Eventually, physical words are no longer adequate to describe what you discover is already there within you.

Unfortunately, most people will spend their entire life without really starting to explore their inner world. They will never see what is real and simply explore and sustain what is not the primary reality.

This is where that feeling, "There's something missing in my life", comes from. Deep down you know there is a greater reality, a more profound space. It's your own inner spaciousness calling you. When you focus too much on what is 'out there' that innate knowingness of your authentic self makes itself heard in your mind with thoughts like, "I know there is something else', or "I really sense there is more to life than what I see with these eyes".

While the seven practices are covered later, it's appropriate to mention Mindfulness Meditation here, while highlighting where it can lead you. Mindful meditation is essentially an exercise to help you hold your attention on the present moment. To become fully aware of what you are experiencing now, in your body, in your mind, in your interaction with another, in the room ...at this moment now.

That sounds easy but it's not, for most people. We live in the age of distraction. We have developed the habit of escaping the present by hitching a ride on your thoughts, by seeking and becoming addicted to sensation. 'Train of thought' is a good metaphor. We get on the train and then travel through all the carriages, unable to take our seat and just watch the scenery pass by. One carriage, i.e. one set of thoughts, leads to another until we are lost on the train. We all know what it's like to be lost in thought.

Our thoughts are mostly about the past and the future. Some are worry thoughts and others are sad thoughts etc. Mindfulness gets you off the train, so you can stand back from your thoughts. You are then literally out of your mind, so to speak. You return to your center. From there, you simply observe. As you do, not only does your mind become calm but your body also moves into a more balanced state. That's why mindfulness is now 'on the menu' in schools, corporations, prisons and hospitals all over the world. It's a practice that begins to restore mastery of consciousness.

Heartful Meditation

When you start to master the inner art of being a 'detached observer' of your thinking you also start to become naturally aware of deeper feelings. These feelings are of you in your natural state of being. You feel calm, loving, contented, benevolent towards others. As you read these words it may sound like a passive state that is uninvolved and uninterested in anything in the world. But the reality is quite the opposite. Life and work become a context of creativity and play. Free of the tension of wanting and needing anything from anyone, and you are therefore able to give the best of your self without thinking. It's from there that those feelings of meaningfulness and fulfillment arise.

There is also a clarity of intellect, now unclouded by random, rushing thoughts and emotions, that allows you to evaluate and discern what is most useful to give your time and energy to.

Soulful Meditation

Then, gradually, whenever you sit for meditation you slip naturally into your core state of being, which is silent and still. It's where you lose awareness of the changing world and of the passing of time itself. In that inner state your energy, which is you, is at complete rest. Thoughts, images, memories, feelings no longer attract or distract you. No longer are you pulled by them or into them. No longer do you have any sense of worldly identity. This is the ultimate liberation while you're occupying the form that you animate.

Being fully here now is liberation from becoming lost in past and future thoughts and emotions.

It's not that you stay in that state. But it's the nearest you will come to consciously creating an out of body experience while still in the body! When you return and restore your awareness of change and time, action and interaction, you notice you are somewhat refreshed and renewed. Your awareness is a little clearer and your intellect a little sharper each time.

However, the meditative practices won't work so well if you are doing them because you think you 'have to'. The greatest effect is when you sit, out of curiosity and interest, ready to insperience whatever comes up and being open to any feelings that may arise. Any attempt to force, any ambition, indeed any desire to reach any state, only delays its realization. Meditation on its own however, is not enough to get you back on track, as we'll see in when we explore all the practices.

4 If I realize I am no one and have nothing does that mean I should have no ambition and no progress in my life?

Be ambitious. Strive for the stars. It's obviously a personal choice. But if you become more aware of your self and how everything you do starts with your state of being, your state of mind, the state of your intellect, then you naturally realize that the achievement of any ambition in the material world 'out there', is dependent of the quality of your creation within your consciousness 'in here'.

For most people ambition is driven by the illusion that when I achieve my ambition then I will be happy, satisfied, fulfilled. And yes that's 'enough' for some. But they probably won't make the connection between any unhappiness, frustration, dissatisfactions and their ambitiousness. And that's OK too. Making that connection requires a mix of introversion and introspection, usually preceded and instigated by some kind of 'brick wall' moment.

Most worldly ambitiousness is a form of 'desire for me' in disguise. We make that desire respectable by encouraging worldly ambition in each other. But the desire is usually based on the illusion that if I get/achieve what 'I want' then I'll be happy.

The deepest level of ambition might then be defined as the restoration of complete clarity and freedom to ones consciousness. Everything flows from there.

YES BUT...

...how on Earth do these insights translate into the practicalities of daily life?

Well you certainly don't go around telling people I am 'no one' and I have nothing. Well you can, but I wouldn't recommend it for obvious reasons!

These realizations occur silently and subtly within your consciousness. As they do, you continue to play your role/s as you have up to now. However, within your consciousness you are gradually becoming freer. More detached. That does not mean cold or separated or distant. It means outcomes matter less, people's words and behaviors no longer upset you, you lose any neediness from your relationships, you are no longer motivated by the acquisition of ...anything. In other words, you start living from inside out, instead of outside in. You no longer expect the world to give you what YOU want to make YOU happy! You've realized it can't.

Once again, enough words! You cannot know how true this may be until you become curious and interested your self. That means seeing for your self how trying to be someone creates anxiety, trying to sustain the illusion of possession creates anxiety, believing you have be somewhere else or achieve something else creates anxiety. Anxiety is fear and fear is stress and stress is unhappiness. Connect these dots within the reality of your own experience and you will begin know for your self.

As we revisit our leadership profile it becomes obvious why the absence of these three realizations will make it hard, if not impossible, to manifest the appropriate responses and behaviors in any leadership role.

We may have moments when we genuinely display the traits within our leadership profile, but it's unlikely we will be able to consistently demonstrate and enact such traits when we believe we are somebody, when we believe we have possessions to hold on to and protect, and when we believe we are going somewhere or need to arrive somewhere significant. As follows!

RESPECT *everyone you meet, regardless of their history:*

When your sense of self is based on a position or a reputation, you will seek the respect and recognition of others to affirm and bolster your own self-respect. This creates insecurity (fear) and resentment (anger) when you are not respected. You start to doubt your self when people's response to you is not as you would expect or desire.

CELEBRATE *the success and achievements of others:*

If you see someone getting ahead in their life, if it's in any way where you would like to go, or a talent you would like to be recognized for, or if you perceive them being better than you and that bothers you in any way, then you will likely not genuinely celebrate their progress.

ENCOURAGE *others with your effervescent enthusiasm:*

If you are identified and therefor dependent on a position or possessions in any way, the fear of loss or damage will drain your enthusiasm. Your own worries (fears) will not allow you to be authentically and consistently encouraging of others.

AVAILABLE *when others need someone to listen to their story or guide them forward:*

If you are busy playing politics to protect a position, or you are worried about what may happen to what you believe is 'mine' or you are habitually preoccupied with someone or something else you will not be able to be fully present and available for another.

ELEVATE *others by putting them ahead of your self:*

You will find that hard to do consistently when your sense of self, your sense of who you are, is based on what you do or what you have. You will fear losing the possibility of being elevated yourself.

LISTENING *before speaking, to the words and feelings of others:*

You will find that it's almost impossible to listen deeply and fully if your sense of identity is based on believing you are someone important and therefore needs to be heard. You will likely try to solve other's problems instead of allowing them to realize their own solutions, simply because your position, which you mistakenly use to build your sense of self, needs to be affirmed by being seen as the source of solutions and ideas.

EMPATHISE *with others as they go through different challenges:*

When you need to be recognized as a position or role it's not easy to be caring about what is going on within others. That requires giving your full attention to them. But you cannot care about others if you are always thinking and worrying about your self. It isolates you from them in your own mind. Empathy requires the intention to build a state of unity or communion, with the other. Not so easy if you are constantly seeing your self as a position separated from their position.

TRUST *everyone and they feel your trust because you've realized no one can hurt you:*

When you identify with what you do or what you have, then whenever someone judges what you do or what you have, you take it personally and as a slight upon you. That means you feel hurt believing they hurt you. But they didn't, you hurt you (create feelings of hurt i.e. emotions). But now you have a memory of 'they hurt me' so you will not be able to trust them and they will feel that attitude from you.

OPEN *to others point of view, their position, perceptions and desires:*

Whenever you become attached to anything or anyone not only do you use them to build your sense of self but you become closed around what you are attached to. This takes place within your consciousness. So, while you may be open to some people and situations, as soon as they display any threat to what you are attached to, you will become closed. Even if it's just the words they say.

KIND *and generous person who always enquires as to the wellbeing and needs of the other:*

Kindness and generosity require a 'giving consciousness'. When you believe you are someone and that you 'possess things' then you are more often (not always) looking to 'take things' like recognition, appreciation, acceptance etc. Or indeed trying to acquire more material things. This habit diminishes the natural kindness and generosity of your true nature.

ACCEPTING *of others point of view, their attitudes, their behaviors:*

Very difficult if you are opinionated in any way. Opinions mean beliefs and beliefs are 'things' in consciousness that we become attached to. They are a subtle form of possessing. That makes it hard to be open and accepting of other's opinions and therefore ideas and suggestions. Any resistance to other's ideas based on your attachment to your ideas/beliefs will not allow your intellect to assess and evaluate accurately. That, in turn, skews your decision-making.

CO-OPERATION *as you step forward to help, when help is required:*

When you are trying to be someone and acquire more 'stuff' then life becomes competitive. We justify our competitiveness with such ideas and beliefs as 'it's survival of the fittest out there' or 'you always have to take care of number one' i.e. your self'. There may be moments when we 'lend a hand', but often only when it serves our agenda to become somebody important or if it will bring us more of, well, anything and everything!

PATIENCE *with others as you know some need more time and attention than others:*

If you perceive your reputation is dependent on getting something done on time or being somewhere on time, you will likely force your self, and perhaps others, to rush. Patience will be difficult. Impatience then becomes a habit It's not hard to become a rushaholic and a hurry addict. Not exactly a brilliant example for others!

PROACTIVE *as you focus on solutions and not problems:*

Why do so many people become negaholics with their focus on what is always wrong or going wrong or just plain negative? It's often because they perceive so many threats to who they believe they are, what they think they've got or where they think they're going.

HONESTY *when it is required to inform others exactly what you think and feel:*

It's obviously hard to be honest with others when one is not honest with oneself. To believe you 'are someone' and that you 'possess something' are the ultimate lies we have learned to tell our self. They are in the way of our self-honesty and therefore honesty with others. But it's unlikely we will be aware of this as it now seems to be completely normal to want to be someone special, accumulate more material possessions and always be planning to go somewhere.

Only when the penny drops and the realization occurs that 'I am no one' and 'I have nothing,' in reality, do these insights into ones self start to influence how we live our life and how we will lead others.

It's not that you drop everything, give up the day job and head for the cave in the hills. Quite the opposite. Along with these realizations comes an understanding of why everyone else is struggling with their life, perhaps suffering in their life. Yes, there may be physical pain but any mental/emotional suffering is seen and understood to be self-created entirely because 'they' believe, "I am somebody or need to be seen as somebody special" and they believe, "I need more of, well, everything, to live my life happily and successfully".

To lead them, by example, by 'showing' them the way out of their struggles, out of whatever stress they are creating for themselves, then becomes the imperative and possibly the highest, yet most subtle, level of leadership. They may not want or accept that help. They may not be ready to listen and receive verbal guidance, which may just sound like an another ideology to them. But words only represents a very small proportion of a leadership role in this context.

It's only by 'showing' how it is possible to live, be content, be kind, be caring, be natural, while holding and living by what appears to be this radical self-awareness that it's possible to lead others out of their struggle and their suffering.

Is it really possible to 'walk the talk' of such radical truths in an organisational, commercial, market driven, competitive environment? Why not? Maybe not in all such environments. But we still need to pay the bills, put food on the table, take physical care of a family, look after our own physical health. So why not? There is obviously no single right way to do that. Just your way, your choices, your creative application of three of the deepest possible realizations we can have about our self. You will only know when you experiment, review, join the dots between insight and behaviour, notice where and when you compromise your self and perhaps fall into old habits that regenerate your own stress and your particular forms of unhappiness. All self created remember, when you forget you are no one, have nothing and go nowhere!

You may even start to laugh, quietly, to your self, as you notice everyone is running around trying the be someone, trying the acquire more and more, trying to be somewhere where they are not, as you realise how deeply embedded and how widespread these illusions have become. Then again, maybe won't ...start to laugh!

So how would you appear to others as you walk this walk? You would be a lot less tense and anxious as you realise you no longer need to defend or depend on a particular position or job. No one would be able to trigger any upsetness as you no longer identify your self with anything that is not you. Any attacks i.e. judgments or criticisms of what is not you would no longer bother you. Your easiness would be noticed and be at the heart of your ability to influence others with your growing wisdom, as opposed to your previous emotional reactions.

You would struggle and strive a lot less as your ambition to achieve anything in the world will have been demoted in your list of priorities. You now know that any worldly achievement is not what generates happiness or wellness of being. You would therefore have more time for others. Not just those in your immediate physical family but those beyond your immediate circle. You may even sense a pull to be of service to a wider circle as the real meaning of 'servant leadership' becomes more apparent.

In such relationships you would certainly seem more available as you consciously practice 'presence', having realised you can't really be anywhere else other than 'here'. Material possessions will have lost their lustre at all levels. Yes you are still surrounded by material things, but now the fear of loss is gone, the fear of not getting 'more' is gone, the fear of others getting something before you is gone. So worry and anxiety cease to visit head or heart.

As the fears, angers and sadnesses subside they are replaced by a lightness and playfulness that charm, alongside a quiet acceptance of everyone as they are and the world as it is. There is an abiding appreciation for the gift of being able to participate in the lives of others and indeed life itself. Such a simple gift that you could not see before as the busyness of trying be someone and get more somethings occupied your consciousness. That appreciation is then felt by others as a natural grace and humility that you carry into everything you do and bring to every relationship you create.

THE PRACTICES

...and the Art of Becoming Real

There are essentially seven invisible CREATIONS within your consciousness every day.

Thoughts
Feelings
Evaluations
Decisions
Actions
Memories
Habits

Each is shaped and influenced primarily by who you believe you are, what you believe you have and where you believe you are going or want to go. If you don't 'know' and allow the truth regarding each of these 'ideas' to shape your creation, then your creation will not be accurate. It won't be right or wrong, just not accurate. The sign that it's not accurate will be the generating of an emotional state where emotion is a 'disturbance' in and of your consciousness i.e. you!

When your creation is accurate, which means it's aligned with your natural state of being, what you could call your 'trueness', there is no emotion. But your feelings will be warm, rich and deep.

It's likely been a long while since our creations were accurate. In other words, it's been a long time since we were stress free, without suffering and intuitively felt sure we were on the accurate track in our life. That's because of habit. The inaccuracies in our creative process become habitual.

Thinking is what we are doing almost all the time. You are probably doing it right now. That's why you have a mind. The mind is necessary to give form to our thoughts. Thought forms are often referred to as ideas or images. Mostly they arrive out of habit i.e. previously recorded experiences, beliefs, judgments and images. The more we become aware of our thoughts and the more we notice their source the more a master of the process we become. That simply means the more consciously you will be able to choose what to think, which also means you will 'think' a lot less.

Feeling has its origin in consciousness. However, because we are not so self-aware many of us we tend to believe feelings are just physical. Most of us only 'consciously feel' when we are either feeling great, what we call high', or very emotional. Otherwise we have the habit of avoiding, suppressing or trying to alleviate the emotions that we are feeling. Unless they seem pleasurable, such as excitement, which easily becomes addictive. As does fear and anger eventually. Drama queens tend to be emotional addicts.

At this point you may fall into the trap of 'thinking', "Well aren't some emotions negative and some positive?" That's what we learn. But in consciousness, where emotion originates, there is no positive or negative, there is no duality. But that's also another seminar.

Our emotions tend to arrive in our conscious awareness from our subconscious, which is just outside our awareness. They are habitual creations. That's why we often have thoughts and feelings and then think, "Where did that thought/feeling come from?" But the 'I' that says 'I am', that's you, is still the creator.

Emotion is created and felt when a reaction is triggered within our consciousness by something or someone 'out there'. Or when we imagine something 'out there' is going to happen. Our 'feelings' of care, calm and contentment are not emotions. They are our natural state of being. We 'feel' them when we are in such states. Unfortunately, we don't create and feel them that frequently because of the habit of re-creating old emotions. Emotion is a disturbance of our consciousness, as a result of becoming attached to, and identified with, what we are not. That's why all emotions have their origin in the ego and are therefore inaccurate. But don't tell Hollywood! Or indeed most EQ practitioners!

Love and authentic happiness are not emotions. To many that sounds like a strange idea. Until we mutually understand what we each 'mean' when we use words like 'emotion' and 'love' it's not easy to create a conversation and be on the same page around such topics.

Evaluation is the function of human consciousness that makes us sophisticated. Otherwise known as the intellect. In other words, it's what humans do a thousand times more and deeper than any other species. But only when we do it consciously. Only when we practice doing it and then exercise our 'discernment' on increasingly complex issues does our ability to evaluate 'sharpen'.

That's when you notice you are 'seeing' with greater depth and clarity. Often referred to as in-sight! But for most of us our ability to discern, to see with depth and clarity, has become lazy. We've been told what to think, what decisions to make, what choices to engage in, and how to live our lives. Laziness was inevitable. I was lazy, I am still lazy, but I am not half as lazy as I used to be!

Signs of this laziness of the intellect include high levels of stress, difficulty making decisions and many non-discerning, reactive, emotion filled habits.

'Evaluation making' only happens efficiently and effectively (accurately) when it arises from clear discernment, which is only possible when there is the absence of emotion. Most of our decisions are habitual and keep us within our comfort zones, even when such zones are uncomfortable! That's one of the effects of having a lazy intellect.

Action originates, like everything else, within your consciousness, not in your body. Action starts in your mind with images and ideas. Sometimes with conscious choices, more often with habitual choices, that are therefore automatic. Most of our actions are reactions. If there is to be an aim, an ambition for our self, it is to awaken our awareness to our creative process to such an extent that we can no longer be 'triggered' by external events and people. Then our actions can become 'consciously chosen responses'. Responses that are natural, yet completely accurate, informed and shaped by our wisdom and not emotion.

Remembering is the ability to record everything we think, feel, decide and do. That happens whether we want to or not. Everything you have ever thought, felt and done is recorded in your consciousness, in what is known as the subconscious, which is outside your moment-to-moment awareness. If we were fully aware of all the recordings, all the memories of what we have thought, said and done, we'd go crazy with the mental noise!

One of the reasons why a practices such as meditation can help is the process of allowing what is in the subconscious to become conscious. We all know the iceberg principle. 10 percent is visible and 90 percent invisible. Similarly, 10 percent of your consciousness is conscious awareness and 90 percent is subconscious i.e. almost all the recordings in your consciousness are outside your conscious awareness.

As you meditate you lower that line as you become increasingly aware of what is buried in your subconscious. For most of us, what is buried is easily 'triggered' into life and it weighs heavy. This is what is known as 'your karma' i.e. recordings of the physical, mental and intellectual actions, recorded and then buried in your subconscious. Meditation allows you to see and clear what is buried that has been creating feelings of heaviness within you. That's why, with the integration of meditation in one's life there is a gradual increase in the 'lightness of being'. It's similar to slowly emptying the hard disc in your computer thereby freeing up space for new files.

Habit is a collective recording within consciousness which combines the recordings of thoughts, perceptions, beliefs, emotions and behavior. Sometimes just one word can trigger a habitual reaction. All our habits make up our unique personality.

The following practices will disrupt your habitual and inaccurate creations, facilitate a deeper awareness of the real you and start to restore accuracy to your creativity.

There are seven specific practices that allow you to realize *I am no one, I have nothing* and *I am going nowhere*. As these insights become more real within you, they naturally affect and influence the seven aspects (above) of your day-to-day creativity.

Those practices are: (not necessarily in this order).

Meditation
Contemplation/Reflection
Application

Contribution
Company
Curiosity
Playfulness

1 Meditation restores your awareness of your true underlying nature (as outlined at the end of the last chapter). Which means you elevate the vibration of the energy of your consciousness. You begin to restore your ability to vibrate and radiate as what we call peace (being relaxed and calm about everything) as love (being caring and compassionate towards everyone) and happiness (being contented and easy about what's happening around you in the world). Meditation can enhance the quality of your inner life as well as the quality of everything you create within your consciousness.

2 Contemplation and Reflection means what we used to call 'studying' at school. But in the context of your consciousness i.e. you, it's not an academic endeavor.

Contemplating the wisdom of others; reflecting on and realizing the significance of one's own experiences and insperiences; allowing your self to be open to deeper insights; seeing and understanding the creative process of your own consciousness; are all part of contemplation and reflection. The result is a growing ability to discern deeper meaning and access your innate wisdom, which then enhances the quality, appropriateness and effectiveness of all that you create i.e. your thoughts, feelings and decisions.

3 Application means putting into practical action the insights and realizations that occur as the result of meditation, contemplation and reflection. As you become more self-aware so you become more honest with your self, which means you hide and suppress less. This also allows you to create more intimate relationships where the real meaning of intimacy is defined by how open and connected (without becoming attached) you are in your relationships with others.

4 Contribution means the giving of your energy without wanting or expecting anything in return. Sounds simple and even obvious. However, in reality, it goes against all that we have been taught and recorded in our consciousness. It's as if we have been programmed to acquire as much as we can from others, both tangible and intangible.

Our happiness and security are mistakenly tied to acquisition and possession when, in reality, that is the cause of unhappiness and insecurity. This is fully realized in the process of meditation and contemplation. Creating and affirming the intention 'to give', without making our happiness and security dependent on some form of return, is liberating. Not to mention a vital ingredient in forming real relationships with others.

5 Company means deliberately seeking and gravitating towards people who are also interested in what's going on within consciousness and therefore also within other practitioners. The process of conversation and mutual exploration helps you to sustain your interest as well as triggering new and deeper insight into what is going on within you. Avoiding, where possible, toxic relationships, becomes a sensible and obvious thing to do, in order to stop being colored darkly by the company of those who tend to project a victim mindset. Until, that is, you are spiritually strong enough to remain 'undisturbed' by the darkness of others.

6 Curiosity is the red thread that runs through the six previous practices. Unless there is a genuine curiosity, an interest and intention to see more deeply, know with greater clearly and become more real, then the five practices tend to become exercises that we think we 'have to' do as opposed to want to do.

People tend not to change until they are ready. Readiness is normally defined by their level of suffering or discomfort. If you have set your self up with what you believe is a comfortable life, and it's been that way for a while, it won't be long before you start thinking about such practices, "Do I really need to do this?"

You may even answer to your self, "Yes I do", but if you are firmly in your comfort zone and any stress is still tolerable, the conviction may be likely to fade. Especially as you start to notice how each one of these practices itself may induce some discomfort ...at first.

7 Playfulness It's easy to let such practices become serious endeavors. As a result we may start to resist or stop the natural playful aspects of our being to emerge. We all have different ways to be playful in our life. It's that playfulness that often allows us to relax, think less, be our self more, and refresh our energy in a different way. Play allows us to be creative and spontaneous while it also induces insights that would not otherwise emerge so easily.

Breaking Out

It's like breaking out of prison. You will notice how and why you are imprisoned by your material comforts and even though there may be some uncomfortable relationships in your prison of comfort, you will have found a way to tolerate them. But getting out of a physical prison requires doing uncomfortable things like digging a deep tunnel, getting your hands dirty, working determinedly and consistently, consciously managing your energy. Your return to your original and authentic nature from which your true character emerges is similar. Your natural state is freedom. But you cannot be free until you cast off what is imprisoning you. Hence 'the practices' and the necessity to find your way of implementation while combining them in ways that work for you.

So **meditation** takes you deeply inside, expands your self - awareness while inducing in-sight. **Contemplation** and **reflection** generate understanding and the meaning of what you find. **Application** is putting into practice what you realize for your self in that process, not what you read here or there. **Contribution** is recognizing life is essentially 'relationship' and we are meant to help each other. Keeping good **company** is the context in which you get to express your experiences of what you are finding inside and, as you do, you see and understand them with greater clarity.

One final seeming paradox. While we talk about changing our self you/I/we, don't actually change. What you create changes. The quality of your thoughts and feelings, attitudes and decisions, perceptions and behaviors, all change. But only when you begin the process of awakening to who you are. Everything flows from there. Beyond and prior to what you create, is the authentic you. Pristine and fully intact, complete and perfect. You are, as you have always been, and will always be. But to restore that state to your awareness and allow it to be the source of your creativity, it's necessary to expose and delete the many learned and assimilate beliefs gathered along the way.

THE SHIFTS

... the art of moving from Force to Power

The fruit of realizing that you are no one, you have nothing and you are going nowhere, are the shifts that occur naturally in all areas of your life. The gradual, yet sometimes sudden, occurrence of these shifts are also signs you are moving in an 'accurate' direction.

When we attempt to maintain the idea in the minds of others that we are someone significant, perhaps someone with substantial possessions (material wealth), we try to 'force' our way through life. Grasping, holding tight and seeking to acquire 'more' of anything are forms of force.

Perhaps you have learned to believe that what you have today (possession) is a mark of your success, your prowess, your ingenuity, maybe even your masculinity or femininity. Have you been attempting to force the world to give you more? More things, more recognition, more approval, more applause - different 'mores' for different people. All of that forcing (wanting, working, manipulating, acquiring, accumulating etc.) comes with tension and anxiety.

But the tension and anxiety disappear when you realise there is no one 'here', in worldly terms, to affirm. There is nothing to hold on to. That's when you start to stand in your power. The habits of forcing atrophy and internal 'shifts' occur as your authenticity reveals itself, which is then a powerful influence for others.

Here are some of those internal shifts. You don't need to announce them, they just happen as you awaken to the reality of who and what you are, which is the result of awakening to the unreality of who and what you are not.

In an organisational context, these are also the main shifts that someone will make in a managerial position as they become an authentic leader. But they are shifts we will all make, in our own way, at our own speed, if we set off down the path described by the practices already mentioned.

Here's the theory. The actuality occurs within you.

1 From OBJECT to PERSON

Do you see people as objects that are there just to get the job/task done? Or do you see them as human beings? Do you see other people as the source of how you see your self? Do you need their recognition and approval? You do! Now you know that's because you are trying to be someone in others eyes. If you see and treat other people as the means to such ends it obviously shapes how you will interact with them, which in turn influences how they will interact with you, and therefore their level of commitment to you as a leader.

That means you will be beholden in some way to others. That's not someone standing in their power. It's a weak position in any relationship. But the moment you end that neediness by realising who and what you are you step back into your power. The habits of resentment, blame and judgment fall away. The perception of 'them' as people replaces the perceptions of them as a 'function', as a 'source', as a 'resource'. Respecting and accepting them as a human being changes the nature and the dynamic of the connection as the relationship itself becomes more real.

2 From TELLING to ASKING

Do you find your self in 'telling' mode more than 'asking' mode? It's often a sign you are trying impose your self, which a form of force, in order to be recognised as someone significant, someone who 'knows best'. Whereas, when you ask with a genuine curiosity, with the intention to value the other's perceptions, with the motive to empower others, then you stand in your power.

By releasing any impatience to get answers and asking deeper and deeper questions around any issue, you expand your awareness of the many dimension of an issue and begin to see the real root cause. For example, why are there so many drugs on the streets, leads to the question why do so many people become prey to addiction, leads to the question what is it in our culture or education that makes people so vulnerable, leads to the question what is the quality of parenting, which may lead to the question why don't we have formal parenting classes in every town etc. etc.

Notice the temptation to stop and answer the question. Opinions often abound as we seek recognition for our 'intelligence' in order to be seen as 'someone significant' by others. Arguments often ensue. And the opportunity to dig deeper, see deeper, contemplate deeper, is missed.

3 From CONTROL to INFLUENCE

Being controlling is obviously a sign of forcefulness as you try to get others to do what 'I want'. Yet, relationship at any level in any context is built out of the mutuality of influence. To be a powerful influence in a set of relationships requires the openness to be powerfully influenced one's self. Otherwise others will become closed to you.

Do you become frustrated or upset with people? Do you find your self thinking, "They must ...They should...They have to..." That means you still believe you can control what you cannot control. You still believe that the world 'should' dance to my tune! That means you are not allowing your self to realise new and creative ways to influence.

4 From RESISTANCE to ACCEPTANCE

Do you react emotionally to other people? When you do it's usually a sign of resistance. That means you are using force to either avoid what you don't want or manipulate your way to what you do want. Many live their entire life in an almost perpetual state of resistance. Therefore some form of anxiety and tension is almost always present within their consciousness. Not such a wise way to live, and certainly not someone standing in their power.

Power is demonstrated when you choose to accept others as they are, accept situations as they arise and accept circumstances as they unfold. That's not to say you agree, or acquiesce, or condone. Acceptance is the first step towards being a guiding influence in any situation.

It signals the end of any habitual 'emotional reactions' and a sign there is a growing wisdom around how to embrace and influence all that occurs in our presence. Not influence what's on the news or the people and events that inhabit the content of our cappuccino conversations, but whoever and whatever is in our immediate vicinity.

5 From COMPETITION to CO-OPERATION

One of the leader's greatest dilemmas or challenges is between creating a 'culture of co-operation' while operating in a wider 'context of rampant competition'. Many, if not most of us, are conditioned to believe life is a competitive journey. From this belief comes the belief that we need to 'acquire' more in order to be comfortable today, secure in our future and be seen to be strong and successful in our life.

Competition is glorified, as sport becomes the ultimate entertainment and a drug we are now prepared to pay premium subscriptions to be delivered to the screens in our living rooms.

Acting from a belief that competition is how life works is a forceful way to achieve, acquire material success and build a reputation. It comes with much suffering in the form of tension and anxiety, fear and resentment. Not mention the inevitable moments of loss.

Yet, deep down we also know that co-operation is more natural, some would say necessary, mode of living. It's when we share our power, enhance each other's capabilities and get things done together. How we live is, for some, defined by this choice - do I compete my way through life or co-operate and build co-operative relationships in my life? It's a question that is always worthy of a creative conversation.

6 From SURVIVAL to SERVICE

Have you grown up with the popular belief that life is survival of the fittest? It's an idea that often becomes the rudder that guides how we shape our career. This means constant fear usually in the form of anxiety. The fear of not surviving the job, not surviving a particular relationship, not surviving specific encounters, which then sabotages our creativity and our ability to relate well with others.

Whereas there are those who have decided their highest purpose is not survival but to be of service to others. In the first instance the belief in survival generates a 'have to' attitude whereas an 'I am here for others' intention tends to generate a 'want to' enthusiasm that cares for others before the self.

'Survival' generates the fear that drains our power whereas the 'service' generates an enthusiasm that empowers. This is why asking questions like why am I here, what am I here to do, how do I create a meaningful life, eventually leads to realizing a sense of purpose that shapes your intentions and infuses them with the wisdom and power of your own consciousness.

7 From SLAVERY to MASTERY

Are you a slave or a master? Most of us are slaves most of the time. It's just how the world has influenced us. It's not wrong or bad, it just is. How do you know?

There are five steps into slavery which we've been conditioned to take and, for many, have become habitual. For example, something gets your **attention** like a new dress or suit. You allow your self to be **attracted** to the dress or suit, then you create a desire. You can't stop thinking about the dress or suit, the object your desire, which is the beginning of **attachment**. You then obtain the object of your desire and indulge in it. You wear it and feel great in it, so you keep wearing it because you feel great, which means you become **addicted**. And, as any addict who has come out the other side of their addiction will tell you, there has to be an **atonement**. For the drug addict that means a short visit to a clinic to detox. For the celebrity addicted to the limelight there also needs to be an atonement, a detox process, if they are going to be free and clean.

So the five steps into slavery are:

Attention

Attraction

Attachment

Addiction

Atonement

The suit or dress are simply examples. Take a moment and identify what or who you are attached to and you will find your addictions. We all tend to be addicted to something or someone. Then trace it back to the moment it/they got your attention and follow the process from there. Please don't call it love!

Whereas the path of the master i.e. being the master of what you create within your self, looks like this.

You **dis-identify** with anything, anyone or anywhere. This allows you to remain **detached** from all ideas, images, beliefs and memories. That allows your energy, the energy of consciousness, to be free to do the most important internal action, which is **discern.** This is the process of evaluation of the quality of an idea, of what is true from what is false, what is real from what is illusory, what is high quality from what is low quality. The master needs to be able to do this because each and every day you need to make many **decisions.** And decision-making is dependent on how free you are from attachment. And because there is no attachment there will be no emotion to distract and cloud your intellect, your attention, which is you. That means you can remain **determined** to carry out your decisions through the appropriate action/behavior. To terminate is to end, to de-terminate i.e. be determined, is to never end until the decision is fully enacted.

So the five steps into mastery are:

Dis-identification

Detachment

Discernment

Decision

Determination

The transition from slavery to mastery doesn't happen instantly. It tends to happen slowly, over time, with practice, with awareness, with the occurrence of many AHA moments. Only when you have arrived does it seem to have happened 'so fast'.

8 From BELIEFS to VALUES

You can never know if your beliefs are true. Belief must always be accompanied by doubt simply because to say, 'I believe' is also to say, 'I don't know'. But that does not stop many of us from arguing as if our beliefs are absolute truths. To argue is to attempt to force one's beliefs onto and into another. In the process of such attempts we create frustration and anxiety and thereby drain our power.

Whereas, the more enlightened individual never argues for two reasons. First, they have realized beliefs are static 'things' in consciousness. They become deeply held personal attachments. Sometimes not so deep! Whereas the reality of life and living is dynamic, ever flowing and shifting.

Second, the reality of life, some might say the truth about life, cannot be limited by ideas and concepts or by the spoken word. Words can only point but never capture. Induce perhaps, but never contain. Someone who 'knows' this does not waste time and energy in trying to convince anyone of anything. That means 'emotional reactions' can never be triggered by the beliefs or ideas of others.

They also know that 'values' are not things or ideas or concepts. Value is, in the reality of relationship, a verb, not a noun. When we make a noun and give a name to a value we try to make it a static 'thing' in our consciousness. That's when we might say, "My values are...", then reel of a list of 'things'.

To value is something we do. Value is 'ascribed' within consciousness and demonstrated by behaviour. Ascribed value is implicit in attitude, words and behaviours towards anyone or anything. Mostly it's a subconscious habit, usually the result of the conditioning of parents and society. The fully awakened being ascribes value to everyone and everything, as they know that everyone and everything is of great value. To an enlightened soul the idea of human worthlessness is extinct.

We tend to make our values and belief/s ideas and concepts that we hold and possess. This is 'my belief". These are my values. Whereas valuing, in its truest sense, is not something to be held. It is ever moving from me to you. I may say "I respect you", and as I do, I am ascribing value to you, within me. The same with care and empathy, guiding and helping. Implicit in any of those intentions and behaviors is me saying 'I value you'.

In this way, we use the power of our consciousness to give 'value'. When you do that, 'authentically', you may notice, it empowers you first and foremost.

Clever design!

By the way...

You may have noticed the frequent use of the word 'accurate', where most would use 'right or wrong'.

But in consciousness there is no right or wrong. There is no duality. In society, it's necessary to specify right and wrong behaviors and have laws that enforce. Otherwise chaos would likely ensue. But in consciousness there are simply different points of view OR different viewing points. Such points of view are always shifting, from moment to moment, depending on many factors. Not least when you awaken to the reality of your authenticity.

There is however, 'accuracy'. That refers to everything you create, from your perception to your attitude to your behavior. And what you create within consciousness depends to what extent you are being your true, authentic self.

When you restore your authenticity you will see for your self exactly why there are no rights and wrongs within ...you! You will also come to know how accurate your creation is simply by what you feel.

If you feel in any way 'emotional' then some degree of accuracy has been lost. Fortunately, such loss is always temporary. But it takes time to 'see' this for your self. One reason is we seem to have no clear sense and shared meaning around 'emotions' and 'feelings'.

When your creation (thoughts, attitudes, perceptions etc.) are aligned with, and arise out of, your authentic self i.e. your true nature, there is no emotion. Just a feeling of peacefulness and contentedness and a quiet self created sense of meaningfulness and fulfillment.

But don't tell Hollywood!

Part TWO

The Outer Journey

101
Leadership
NUDGES

Turning Insight into Practice

It seems people seldom change after reading a book, attending a workshop or listening to a podcast. They may acquire useful, even inspirational information, but only personal knowledge, gained through a process of self-realization, restores the accurate awareness of one's self and thereby alters character and personality.

You already know all that is written here. That's why, as you read, you may think to yourself, "Yes, I get that, I knew that, that's not new!"

But are you doing it, living it, practicing it? Have you plumbed the depths of this or that particular dimension or that particular aspect ...for your self! Have you gone beyond information and accessed your own knowingness, then allowed that to empower a change in your behavior?

The purpose of the following pages is to highlight some of the many dimensions of the character and competencies necessary to be a leader of others. Then, to challenge you to 'see for yourself' by engaging with the questions relevant to that dimension.

The aim is to NUDGE you towards exploring, developing and realizing your own depth. And then to challenge you to act. If you do not act on what you realize for yourself you miss the opportunity to become more competent.

How best to use each NUDGE?

- Ideally you will need a journal in which to write your reflections and responses to the questions at the end of each Nudge.

- The journal is also useful for your own contemplation on any issues or problems you believe you are facing.

- Take one nudge per week. Focus on that particular aspect of your behavior or perception or relationships.

- Take some time out - ten minutes here, five minutes there - in a quiet corner to 'contemplate and scribble' - write your results, insights, reflections and decisions as you progress through the week.

- You can follow the sequence of the Nudges numerically or you can put the numbers 1 to 101 in a jar and allow the universe to choose what you will focus on for the coming week as you pull one out of the jar at the start of each week. Or perhaps ask someone close to give you a number between 1 and 101 for the week.

After nearly two years you should have enough material in your journal to construct your own leadership course, if not before! By then, you will have accumulated many 'real time' experiences and realizations, probably many examples and stories to tell and cultivated your own leadership wisdom.

Integration of the Inner with the Outer

As you proceed with this, the outer aspect of the journey, try to keep referring back to the insights on the inner journey in part one.

Remember, such radical insights are not implying you give up the 'day job' of living and being part of a team or family. But allowing such insights to come through the way you create your thoughts and feelings and the ways in which you connect and interact with others.

The more you realize for your self what we explored in part one the more your character becomes authentic and the less of a personal agenda you will have in your relationships. But above all the better you will 'feel' within your self and about your self.

Yes, there will be a few 'glitches' along the way, depending on your journey so far. But that, as they say, is par for the course!

If anything is not clear feel free to email me
at any time at mike@relax7.com

Living Leadership

In the universe of organizations manager is a position whereas leadership is an attitude.

'Manager' may appear on your business card but 'leader' only appears in the minds of others when THEY decide to follow you.

You can't 'make' anyone follow you. If you try you will likely disappear as 'leader' in their minds.

Manager is 9 to 5, leadership is 24/7.

Managers manage tasks, leaders lead people.

Sometimes separating the two is not so straight forward.

Ultimately there is only one way to lead people and that is by example.

There is always someone watching. And if someone isn't watching, you are. At least retrospectively.

Are you the same in private as you are in public? Would observers see the same behaviors? If there are any private inconsistencies they will likely become apparent publically.

Setting an example is one thing, maintaining it is another!

Question: In your role as a leader what do you think is the most important quality people should observe in your behavior?

Reflection: If someone were to follow you all day with a video camera what would they see are your three main flaws and three main strengths?

Action: Write down the names of three people who work for you and then what you think each person needs to see in you, and therefore receive from you, which would help them.

Deeper Questions

It's often more effective to ask the right questions than have all the answers.

Fresh questions can stimulate new and often transformative insights.

Questions can help people drop their biases that can often block creativity within conversations.

Questioning, not out of resistance but out of curiosity, fosters the development of deeper and more creative thinking.

Creating progressively deeper questions together can generate a stronger culture of collective problem solving and truth seeking.

Instead of instantly seeking solutions and answers to problems, a short process of asking different questions around the issue generates a deeper understanding of the various influences involved.

By inviting the team to find and articulate the right questions it also pulls them out of their comfort zone.

The leader knows that by sharing the problem and asking for deeper questions they are involving the team and valuing their input. This strengthens the connections within the team,

Question: Currently, what are the two most challenging issues you are facing personally?

Reflection: Instead of trying to find a solution take some time and generate questions around each issue.

Action: In the next team meeting invite the team to generate questions around an issue that the team is currently facing.

Strange Attractor

When scientists force a 'sponge fish' through a sieve it breaks into hundreds of parts.

But when they leave the parts to float in the water they slowly come back together and reform.

They don't know why or how, but they call the invisible energy that enables this the 'strange attractor'.

Sometimes, in teams, the manager is not the real leader. The real leader is one of the team members who seems to be attracting others more than the manager.

The wise manager, who is ostensibly the leader, is not phased by this.

They neither feel jealous nor threatened. They set out to lead the person who is the 'strange attractor', and through leading them they lead the team.

The enlightened manager welcomes such an individual and brings them 'on side' allowing them to be the 'defacto leader' of the group in many situations.

Question: Is there anyone in your team who is obviously attracting the attention and the followership of others more than you?

Reflections: How could you work with them and through them to lead the team. Managers manage tasks, leaders lead people. Are you leading or managing?

Action: Create a plan to empower that person progressively. At this weeks team meeting ask the question, "Why are we all leaders for each other"? And then facilitate an open discussion.

Change Ready

The general response to change at any level, including
tasks/processes/systems, is likely to be one of resistance from
some, if not the majority.

Anything that threatens a comfort zone will tend to illicit a fearful
response.

But if you allow time for discussion, exploration and acceptance
of what is proposed, it gives others the time and space adjust
their comfort levels.

Once the new ways are understood and mentally integrated it
becomes easier to accept them in reality.

It's obviously wise to introduce some changes slowly and others
rapidly.

Much depends on your judgement of each individuals readiness,
willingness and ability to handle change.

Question: What specific changes are in the pipeline that may
affect the stability of individuals and the team?

Reflection: The only unchanging certainty in life is that there will
always be change. However, while people are resistant to
change they are also addicted to change. What's the difference?

Action: Create a map and appropraite timeline for what you
perceive to be all the necessary forthcoming changes that will
have to take place to move the organisation/team forward.
Facilitate the creation of a 'vision' of what the changes that are
coming will look like.

Respect All

It is wise to have no favourites amongst those who would follow you.

There is the understanding that, over a period of time, a show of favouritism or the giving of special attention to one person can 'trigger' negative thoughts and attitudes in others.

Favouritism is a form of attachment that easily leads to over familiarity, grows into a subtle dependency, which can then compromise your integrity.

Much better to respect all equally, regardless of the behaviours and attitudes of each member of the team.

This is not so easy as many of us grow up with the idea that respect has to be earned and can be easily lost.

The enlightened leader however, has realised that every human being is worthy of respect, regardless of their past action or present intentions.

However, the past actions or present intentions may not be worthy of the same respect as the person. That's why it's necessary to separate the person from the actions/intentions.

The leader in any relationship is the one who maintains their respect for the other, for all others, at all times.

Question: Which particular individual/s do you tend to favour in your team and what effect does that have on others?

Reflection: In what ways does your favouring individuals affect your a) respect for others b) your decisions and c) your attitudes?

Action: Ask someone you trust for honest feedback on this subject in relation to the way you manage/lead your team.

Self Management

One of your daily priorities is the maintenance of your own 'consciousness'.

This means 'self-management' - not in a self-serving or self-obsessing way, but to cultivate self-awareness, self-renewal and self-motivation.

You know the value of taking regular time to consciously clear the clutter of your mind and sharpen the focus of your intellect.

By keeping the mind calm and unruffled by emotion you also enhance the quality of your creativity.

By fine-tuning the ability of your intellect to maintain focus and clarity you make wiser decisions and build better relationships.

Take regular 'time out' to *meditate/contemplate* as you train your mind to remain calm.

As you *reflect/review* your own 'insperiences' you increase your intellect's depth of insight and wisdom.

Question: What are the different functions of the mind and what are the different functions of the intellect?

Reflection: What are the main influences on the minds capacity to be calm and the intellects capacity to discern clearly?

Action: Take five minutes each day this week to consciously rest your mind. Then take five minutes to objectively reflect on a current issue that is not clear. During either practice, if you feel any emotion arising then step away from it internally, observe it, until it subsides, and then return to your reflective practice.

Emotional Intelligence

At the heart of all social skills is the 'feeling state'.

What you are feeling will shape your thoughts and behaviours, and therefore the quality of your interactions.

Everyone gets stressed. It's different things for different people in different situations, that 'trigger' the emotions of stress.

When one is 'feeling emotional' it is signalled by 'reactive behaviour'. This is what makes individuals unpredictable, sensitive and often inconsistent.

That's why your consistency and calm, clear headedness and the ability to always be proactive, is dependent on:

a) your awareness of your emotions

b) your acceptance of full responsibility for your emotional state.

c) your ability to disempower your emotions and restore your calm and clarity

Otherwise, emotionally driven behaviour can sabotage a relationship that has taken a long time to build.

One emotional reaction can be like the momentary lighting of a match that destroys, in minutes, a hundred year old redwood tree...metaphorically speaking!

Question: To what extent would you consider your self to be emotionally intelligent (percentage)? What would you need to do to increase that intelligence?

Reflection: You are 100% responsible for ALL your thoughts and ALL the emotions that you feel. If not, why not?

Action: Ask the team to what extent the team is emotionally aware and accepting of personal responsibility.

EGO Free

The 'primary barrier' to innovation, change, growth and the development of individuals, teams and organisations, is one thing, the ego.

Ego is the creation of a false sense of identity.

It occurs when the you become attached to, and identified with, anything, including objects, people, beliefs or memories.

When you stop making the common mistake of creating a sense of who you are out of what you are not, then people and events cease to be able to trigger an emotional reaction.

The most common attachments in the workplace are position, pay, privileges and possessions.

As a result of being a little more detached from these things you can no longer be threatened by anyone or any event.

You gradually become stress free. You are gradually able to remain internally stable' regardless of what is happening around you.

This allows you to be more available to coach, guide and mentor others.

Question: What is it that you tend to become attached to within your workplace context?

Reflection: Take a moment to reflect and see how any stress you are currently or frequently 'feeling' is connected to something that you are attached to.

Action: Practice the art of detachment from everything and everyone for one whole day. Then take 5 minutes at the end of the day and ask your self what you learned a) about yourself b) about others c) about your circumstances. (remember – non-attachment does NOT mean you do not care or that you disengage or avoid)

Inner Tutor

Realise the value of your intuition.

By regularly taking time out to practice moments of mindfulness.

In such moments, you develop the ability to be the detached observer of your thoughts and memories, cease all worry, and still your mind in the present moment.

In such silent moments, you are then able to hear the quiet voice of your intuition (inner tutor).

This is the voice of your innate wisdom, the wisdom of the heart.

It is a wisdom that can never be lost, only ignored, can never be destroyed, only crowded out by the distracting noise of too much thinking.

In learning to listen and apply this wisdom you will gradually learn to trust and follow your feelings.

Question: Why are feelings more important than thoughts?

Reflection: Have you ever listened to, trusted and flowed with your intuition (your feelings) on an important issue? What was the issue? What was the outcome?

Action: Create three 'pause moments' of three minutes, each day this week, and allow your mind to 'be quiet'. Don't force, just watch. In the watching you will notice that even if your mind is still busy, you are not!

Creative Resource

While people are not just 'human resources', each person carries a spark that is vital to any organisation.

That spark can be found 'within' the consciousness of each individual.

While raw materials, human labour and energy have been perceived as the key resources of all organisations for the last two hundred years, with technology added only recently to that list, that spark represents the energy of ideas.

In a fast-changing world requiring continuous flexibility, adaptation and innovation, the driver and the fuel of that flexibility and change is 'new ideas'.

The leader recognises one of their primary roles is as the facilitator of those ideas from within the minds of others (creativity) and then to empower them to put those ideas into action (innovation).

When people are invited to be creative and to contribute their ideas it also enhances their sense of self value!

Question: What are the best ways to facilitate others creativity in the context of your workplace?

Reflection: Why do people feel they are of greater value when they are being creative?

Action: Create a space and a creative process by which others can offer their ideas sometime this week.

Aligned Leader

It is your role to ensure the teams values, goals and behaviours are aligned with the goals and values of the organisation.

However, some members of the team may only fully commit to following when they sense that alignment within your character and actions.

They will follow only when they sense your 'authenticity of character' based on the consistent alignment of 'right intention', values, words and action.

This inner alignment has its foundation in integrity i.e. the 'integratedness' of your character.

This is possible when you:
a) have a high degree of self-awareness
b) are not serving your own personal agenda
c) you help each member of your team to align with the values of the team.

Only then will you attract a genuine 'following' that will, in turn, allow the smooth integration and collaboration of the various 'characters' within the team.

Question: What is character?

Reflection: As you look at those who follow you how many do so because of your 'character' as opposed to your position? Write a list of your team members and contemplate each one's motives to follow you.

Action: Ask three people this week how aligned and integrated they perceive you to be!

Servant Leader

The servant leader recognises their purpose is to be of service to those for whom he/she has accepted responsibility to lead.

The servant leader does not seek to '*get the best out of*' others (exploitation) but to help others to '*bring the best out from within*' themselves (empowerment).

In doing so they recognise and meet the needs of others before they meet their own needs.

While serving others, which means caring about and empowering others, they recognise they cannot sustain this unless they also care for and refresh their own mind and intellect.

Thus, the foundation of the servant leader is built on parallel tracks - a balance between taking care of one's self while serving others.

Taking care of one self is not taking care of the body's diet, exercise and rest. The body is not the self! The body is the vehicle for the self. It too requires the appropriate nourishment.

Taking care of 'self' requires quiet time, the practice of calm and the contemplation of wisdom.

Question: Why do you think some managers, indeed some people, do not recognise their primary task is to be of 'service' to others?

Reflection: What would you say are the first three steps in being of service to someone who follows you?

Action: Write down what you currently perceive as the primary needs, at this moment in time, of each member of your team?

Self Esteem

You have a major role in helping each member of your team build and strengthen their self-esteem.

Most people are taught to make their self-esteem dependent on the approval/acceptance of others or on external achievements.

This makes them vulnerable to criticism, the withdrawal of approval or failure.

This vulnerability sabotages task efficiency and relationship stability.

Help your team members break their addiction to approval and any neediness in their relationships.

Begin with yourself. Only by understanding and building your own self-esteem can you develop the ability to guide others.

This involves the inner personal work of becoming more aware of your 'intrinsic' attributes which are the basis of your real self-esteem and not the 'extrinsic' feedback/approval of others.

Question: What is self-esteem exactly?

Reflection: In what situations does your self-esteem become vulnerable?

Action: What can you do to build and strengthen your own self-esteem?

Leading Loners

Recognise and accommodate loners.

The loner is that person who prefers to work alone and finds interaction with others difficult, awkward or tiresome.

Don't discourage this trait, it is neither good nor bad.

Don't insist they be a team player or try to force the loner to mix with others.

Affirm it as a strength in the individual and seek ways to help them focus that strength.

See it as the ability to work free of dependency and trust them to complete tasks that require concentrated individual attention.

Paradoxically, the acceptance of the loner's style, and the absence of being forced to be a team player, is what allows them to feel safer in coming closer to, and working with, others.

This tends to happen gradually. Be patient.

Question: Why do you think loners are loners?

Reflection: Most people are addicted to other people... why?

Action: If you are not a loner try being a loner for a day or two and take note of how it feels. If you encounter loneliness ask your self 'what is the difference between being alone and being lonely'?

Artful Motivation

Different things motivate different people.

Some are motivated by rewards, which can range from money to recognition.

Others are motivated by being part of the team or by facing and overcoming the challenge of a new and difficult task.

While many are motivated by their own creativity.

As you become aware of what primarily motivates each member of your team you'll notice that sometimes the greatest indicators of personal motivation are what people do outside the workplace.

By watching what 'lights people up' and asking the right questions you can gradually learn what energises people from inside out AND outside in.

Once identified, try to ensure, as far as possible, that both the tasks and the relationships in the workplace connects to each individual personal motivators.

Question: What motivates you?

Reflection: Is motivation extrinsic or intrinsic – reflect on and discuss with a colleague/s?

Action: List all the people for whom you are a leader, and identify what you think motivates each person. Where you are unsure make a point of engaging them this week and finding out, either directly or indirectly.

Energy Input

Entropy is at work at all levels in the world. Entropy refers to the second law of thermodynamics, which states that all energy in a closed system moves from order to chaos, unless a source of energy comes from outside the system to reinvigorate the energies within the system.

Each day the sunshine comes from outside the eco and bio systems of the planet and replenishes the energy of nature.

Chaos in the energies of the world's climate systems 'seem' to indicate that the sun is not able to replenish physical energy at the same speed as humans are releasing it.

Similarly, with a group, community or team of people. As the team evolves it becomes a closed system in its own subtle ways.

You are the primary source of energy that ensures the teams energy is reinvigorated, refreshed and refocused.

That energy is called enthusiasm. Your enthusiasm is the 'sunshine' for your team. If you are not consistently enthusiastic then you are not leading and it is likely someone else is.

If the team is in permanent chaos, no one is!

Question: How would you describe a) the energy level and b) cohesion level of your team, in terms of percentages?

Reflection: Why do you think your enthusiasm/positivity sometimes fluctuates? Why can chaos sometimes be a good sign?

Action: Create three ways or opportunities to infuse energy and enthusiasm into your team this week.

Four Phases

The group dynamic that most teams go through are well known.

They are:

Forming - learning about each other - when your team is new, roles and responsibilities aren't clear – and everybody is reserved and polite.

Storming - challenging each other – when you start interacting with each other, you become aware that you have different working styles – and conflict begins to arise.

Norming - working with each other - when team members begin to know one another - people start to resolve or accept their differences – and team agreements begin to become part of your team's culture.

Performing - working as one – when your team's structures and process are clear, you can now delegate much of the work – and your team kicks into high performance.

Being aware of where you are now helps you to understand why certain behaviors are currently prevalent.

Being aware of where you are now allows you to realize what may be needed to ease the team into the next phase.

Being aware of where you are now allows you to see and perhaps prepare for what's coming.

Question: In which stage do you think your team is in and why?

Reflection: The transition from one stage to another is never clear or a single moment event – can you sense your team is moving from one stage to the next? If so what are the signs?

Action: Bring the team together and ask each member of the team to reflect and write down in which stage they think the team is in, and why. Then have an open discussion as they share their perceptions.

That Smile

Not long ago science demonstrated that smiling boosted the immune system of the smiler!

The power of a smile can also trigger a boost in the wellbeing of others.

You can use your smile as a way to 'lift the spirit' when the spirit of another is a little down.

Use your smile to convey your personal support when you sense support is needed without the need for words.

When you dispense your smile from your heart, and it conveys a genuine warmth, the energy of joy can be infectious.

As you smile at others you invoke the unbreakable 'law of reciprocity' which reminds you that what you give is what you will get back.

Eventually!

Patience may be required.

Question: Who within your team often needs this kind of 'wordless support' and who could use more of it now?

Reflection: If you find it harder to smile towards some than others why do you think that is? What judgment are you holding on to?

Action: Find five ways to experiment with the law of reciprocity this week!

Failing Forward

Failure is necessary to progress, growth and development.

Organisations and teams that do not tolerate failure have trouble developing new competencies.

Allowing people to experiment with the possibility of failure encourages people to find new ways to make things work more efficiently and effectively.

Fear of mistakes shuts down the 'learning at work' imperative that ensures something new is always emerging.

Fear of risk blocks creativity and stifles team work in ways that discourage people from taking a chance.

Obviously, it doesn't mean there is an excuse to be careless or do just anything. Honest mistakes however, are how most of us learn in the classroom of life.

When the culture has a 'fail forward fast' ethos everyone gets the opportunity to fine tune their discernment of potential new ways, update old ways and kick out the stale.

Accepting there are bound to be moments of failure opens the space for the genius in everyone to flower.

Question: How would you rate the culture of your organisation: Discourages taking a chance for fear of failure = 1 or Encourages experimentation with no fear of failure = 10.

Reflection: Think of three instances where you tried something new and failed – what did you learn in the process?

Action: In what ways could you encourage creativity and innovation by lessening the fear of failure within your team? Brainstorm with the team.

Thick Skin

You will need a thick skin. Decisions have to be made that will not please everyone.

A thick skin is necessary if you are to remain unaffected whenever others attack you verbally. Can you withstand insult and ridicule, passive aggression and back-biting ...without resentment or the urge to take revenge?

Some of these behaviors tend to be the reality, in different ways and to different degrees, in many of today's workplaces.

If you can 'take it' then it means you have a thick skin and such things bounce off, as you stay focused on what needs to be done.

It's useful to understand how sensitive you are and why that sensitivity is present. It depends on how you see your self. (Part One)

The more sensitive you are, the more reactive you will be, the more people will play power games around you and with you. Developing a thick skin is essential in any leadership role.

Scenario

MARY seems to be 'thick skinned' and while this is good in that she is not easily affected by other's comments and judgments, it also means she is not open to other's ideas and does not like to join in anything.

Mary is difficult to approach and make a connection with.

1 What do you think could be the underlying 'issue' (blockage) with Mary?

2 As her manager what would be your AIM in helping Mary develop herself and open-up to others more?

3 What method/s/process would you use in your approach?

Cultivating Followership

People tend to follow a leader for different reasons. One of the most common is admiration, which can sometimes verge on devotion or even worship.

While this may stroke your ego, you also know it will turn sour in the long term.

There will be a behavior or an attitude that does not live up to the someone's image and expectation of you.

You also understand that those who follow out of excessive admiration, worship or devotion often do so at the expense of their own self-respect.

As a result, at some point they will take you off the pedestal. Perhaps followed by the projection of their resentment, maybe anger, onto you.

This means they have not yet fully restored their own self-respect.

Help your people to build and nurture their self-respect and thereby create a deeper more stable relationship.

Which begins with unconditional respect for them.

Question: Whom in your team do you sense follows you out of admiration/devotion?

Reflection: What are the most effective ways to help them break that habit?

Action: Ask each team member who they admire most. Then ask them what it is about that person they so admire i.e. what attributes and qualities. Then help them realize the principle 'what you spot is what you got'!

Attitude Attitude!

When you recognise that leadership is an attitude more than a position, you are always aware of three things.

1 The state of your own being from which emanates
   your attitude - is it reactive or proactive?

2 Discerning the quality of the attitude of others (without judging or labelling them personally) - are they reactive or proactive?

3 Your role in showing others how to become leaders
   by influencing their attitudes through your own attitude.

A true leader is a leader of leaders
not a leader of followers.

By their actions will you *sense* their attitude.

By their intention will you *know* their attitude.

By their example will you *learn* ...attitude!

Question: What is attitude exactly?

Reflection: Attitude transmits way beyond the context in which it is witnessed – how is this so?

Action: What three things can you do this week that will help others enhance the quality of their attitude?

Role Play

Only a lazy manager motivates others to follow by pulling rank and inducing fear.

People may well do what they are told and seem to be being successfully led.

But eventually they are likely to leave a dictator manager, confirming the idea that most people do not leave their organisation, they leave their manager.

But you, as an enlightened leader, build your leadership style based on humility, an unconditional respect for others and the intention to help each one bring the best of themselves to what they do.

Hence, you are able to wear many hats, play many roles, to meet the immediate needs of each team member.

Coach, trainer, teacher, guide, counsellor, mentor, facilitator, are some of the hats you wear in order to encourage and help the team bring the best out of themselves.

The last thing you think or say is therefore, "I am the manager and you should do what I say, or else." Would the same apply to parenting?

Question: Which roles do you currently need to play to help the team?

Reflection: List the skills and capabilities required for each of the above roles.

Action: Experiment with three of those roles this week - bring the best out of yourself while recognizing what you need to learn in order to improve.

Feeling Valued

Can you help every person feel he or she is truly valued?

So that at the end of the day they go home with the feeling they are useful, relevant and significant.

Sometimes you ask for their help. At other times you lean (as in rely) on them. Sometimes you consult them. Then there are moments for inviting their ideas.

Their commitment deepens when they have the feeling they are important to the team and the organisation.

So you ensure every person knows that his or her contribution is of tremendous value.

You know that if you diminish people's worth by ignoring them, taking them for granted, or giving the impression that they are replaceable, they will likely begin to act as if they are less worthy.

Which then easily becomes a self-fulfilling prophecy as they start to switch off and reduce their commitment to the organization.

Do you know how to switch people on and 'up' their levels of commitment?

Question: In what ways can you see and acknowledge the value of an individual's contribution?

Reflection: Recall a time when you felt you were not valued compared to a time when your value was consistently recognised. What difference did it make to you?

Action: Think of one reason you could acknowledge the contribution of each member of the team this week. What is it and when would be the best time to tell them, and where?

Leaders Sense

Can you sense the position that you need to take?

Can you 'sense' when to lead from the front, when to lead by standing alongside and when to lead from behind by putting others in front? And when to make your self scarce?

Sometimes it's necessary to 'take the lead' overtly and make fast but clear decisions.

Sometimes it makes sense to get your hands dirty and muck in with the team as if your just another team member.

Sometimes it's time to put someone else in the hot seat to facilitate the meeting or make the decision.

Sometimes it's best to leave the room, leave the endeavour, and just let them get on with it.

The ability to discern which approach is appropriate at any given moment, comes with experience.

Question: In what ways do you notice yourself seeking the recognition of others as the leader?

Reflection: What would happen if you became a famous leader with a stellar reputation? What would happen if you became an effective leader with little or no recognition?

Action: Identify five present or past situations and 'sense' what might be the leaders most effective position for each i.e. front, alongside, behind or deliberately absent.

Reflective Leader

The world outside is inside!

Regular, quiet reflection on the outer dynamics of the team allows you to discern the factors and the forces that are shaping the teams process and progress.

Relationships can be complex. Sensing and understanding the 'chemistry' between individual team members requires some 'quiet' time.

In such introspective and reflective moments, it's usually best not to 'think' about what you see as much as bring your observations to meet your intuition.

You will be able to 'sense' the true cause of difficult situations and the underlying currents that are influencing the actions and interactions between members of the team.

Then, take that discernment back into your relationship with each member of the team.

Allow it to influence your decisions and interactions. Watch the outcomes. Learn by trial and error.

Questions: How would you describe the current interactive dynamics within the relationships within your team/group?

Reflection: Take a moment to reflect with your inner eye on what you see with your outer eyes. Now what do you 'see' is really going on? Don't stop at any initial conclusions. Keep looking with your inner eye, keep deepening your awareness. Peel back the layers.

Action: What specific actions can you now see are appropriate according to your deeper insights into the team dynamics?

Open Leader

An open and receptive attitude will give people the confidence to trust you and come close.

An open door is the symbol of an open mind, and an open mind is the doorway to an open heart.

An 'open hearted' leader has the capacity to embrace and accept the attitudes and concerns of others regardless of how sharp or negative they may appear.

You can 'accept' without agreeing and still maintain a good relationship!

You remain open because you are unaffected by anything negative that may be directed towards you personally.

Yet you check the validity and accuracy of any feedback received both directly and indirectly.

Question: To what extent is a) your door open b) is your mind open (free of prejudice) c) your heart open? (percentage self-assessment)

Reflection: When your heart opens their hearts will open – why is this so?

Action: Create and enact three key gestures that you could make this week towards your team, that affirms you are open and receptive to all of them.

Risk Taking

As any leader grows into their role they are increasingly prepared to take risks.

By experience they learn to assess the level of 'task risk' and, as they develop their intuitive capacity, they become more aware and sensitive to 'people risk'.

With the result of every risk taken lessons are learned, new insights accumulated and personal wisdom deepened.

In the process of calculating 'risk' the wise leader draws on the experience and wisdom of others, alongside their own realizations as the result of their own reflective process.

In this way they develop an increasingly accurate 'feel' for, and certainty in, the 'risk decisions' that they may make.

Like all these dimensions of leadership in each of these pages each one's approach to the development of any such potential competencies is different, as is the amount of time that is required.

Question: Review and asses 3 of the most recent risks you feel you have taken in the last six months for lessons learned and insights gained.

Reflection: No risk, means no growth, means no change, means stagnation – where have you seen or do you see this process within the work of your team and organization recently?

Action: Identify any current risks that you feel you could take a) with the task b) with people c) with your self.

Finding Strength

One reason why people don't enjoy their work is they are not using their strengths.

One of your first tasks therefore is to find the strengths of each individual, then, as far as possible, to align those strengths to the tasks they do.

In any game, including the game called 'work', all players have a place, a position, where they can play to their strengths and add the most value.

Yes, there are times to play them 'out of position', in order to give each one the opportunity to learn and grow.

But only after some time in their position of strength, which allows them to build their confidence and develop the courage to try something new.

Questions: List your team members and their individual strengths.

Reflection: As you reflect on all the strengths of all members of the team can you see what (skills/abilities) are missing in each one?

Action: Create a plan to teach or provide training of the missing skills/abilities to the relevant team members. Who would benefit from learning which specific skills?

Towards Unity

Your role is to facilitate unity in the group.

Unity cannot be forced and, in some instances, cannot even be suggested, as those who are more comfortable being separate and independent will likely resist the idea.

The first step towards unity is unconditional acceptance of every person, both inside and outside the group. (acceptance does not mean having to agree or condone)

You set the tone, provide the example and initiate the growth of a culture based on unity.

Authentic, consistent acceptance is a form of 'love in action'. Not Hollywood love, but a signal that says, 'I care' about you.

In time, such an intention, and the behaviours that follow, if consistent, melts all barriers and feelings of separateness.

Question: Why do you not fully accept some people inside and outside your team – what lies behind (within you) your non-acceptance? Can you see any general patterns of non-acceptance of 'the other' in your life?

Reflection: Rate your level of acceptance of each member of your team (1 is low and 10 is high) then reflect on each one individually and visualise what you could do to move your self into unconditional acceptance of each.

Action: Take time this week for a one-on-one with each of your team and test the strength of your acceptance of each.

Leadership Qualifications

While you may be a good manager, you may not be such a good leader.

While many managers may spend time and energy gaining academic management qualifications you may have realised effective leadership is not an 'academic' subject.

While managers may study for their MBA the leader is continuously practicing their MBWA (Managing By Walking About).

To an enlightened leader relationship comes before rank and empathy comes before executive decisions in the gaining of others respect and trust.

An effective leader is therefore always 'walking about' refreshing connections, building relationships, setting up subtle lines of open communication.

Inviting input to their decision-making process.

Question: Why is it that the qualities of effective leadership cannot be learned academically?

Reflection: Managers manage things, leaders lead people - the seven reasons 'people' cannot be 'managed' are...

Action: In what ways can you alter your leadership style in order to connect a) more often and b) more deeply with the individuals on your team?

Thoughtful Feelings

In contrasting the difference between a manager and a leader they can often be seen to be opposite ends of the same continuum.

'Manager' tends to signify the more analytical, structured, controlled, deliberate and orderly end of the continuum.

They tend to solve problems and deal with issues rationally.

Whereas the 'leader' tends to occupy the more experiential, visionary, flexible and creative end of the continuum.

They tend to approach problems and issues intuitively.

The 'manager' is the person who more often brings their 'thoughts of the mind' to bear on daily organisational problems/issues. And for the more practical issues this is appropriate.

Whereas the leader tends to bring the 'feelings of the heart' to bear on 'people' issues. They have realised leadership is essentially about winning hearts first and minds ...later!

Question: Is your approach a more thinking or feeling approach as you approach various issues at work?

Reflection: Reflect on the difference between thoughts and feelings – how would you define each?

Action: Write down two current issues at work that are challenging you. In two columns under each issue write your thoughts and then your feelings about each – can you see anything that the two situations have in common?

Future Focus

When you are emotionally intelligent you cease to become upset towards anyone or anything for any reason.

Emotions are realised to be a misuse of personal energy (love/care are not emotions)

Whenever you become upset with anyone or anything, however significant the event or situation may be, it's a sign you are attempting to do the impossible, which is to change the past or other people.

You have temporarily forgotten you are completely responsible only for your self.

When you restore your capacity to accept complete responsibility for your self it allows you to remain free and able to respond proactively regardless of the event/situation.

You know it's a waste of time and energy to dwell on the past.

Whatever has happened is finished, the past has left the building, what is done is DONE... the moment has gone!

You remain stable in the present moment, proactive towards the person/situation and focussed on what's up ahead as you move smoothly into the future.

Question: Who or what do you allow to 'trigger' some form of upsetness in you?

Reflection: Why? And do you accept full responsibility for your upsetness? If not why not?

Action: Take 5 minutes at the end of the day each day this week and review the moments in the day when you forgot your primary responsibility for your 'self'.

Seeing Ahead

While the attention of team members tends to be absorbed by immediate tasks and concerns, and therefore engaged only with what is in front of them at this moment, the leader takes time out and looks ahead.

You see beyond the immediate.

You see the destination clearly (vision) and then confidently and meticulously prepare for the journey (planning).

Your foresight also sees the variety of possible obstacles (anticipation) along the way.

Then, if and when obstacles are to be encountered, they are easily anticipated and surmounted.

While you may occasionally delegate the actual steering of the ship, as an enlightened leader you will frequently involve the team, as a group and individually (consultation), in charting the course.

Question: What are the specific outcomes towards which you are leading your team/organisation/community to achieve?

Reflection: What is IN the way IS the way – why is this true?

Action: List all possible specific obstacles which may arise and how you would deal with each one. Such obstacle could be relationships, events, circumstances etc.

Creative Flexibility

In a fast changing world all systems, processes and structures have an increasingly short shelf life.

You are also less likely to cling to tradition.

You are never attached to yesterdays methods, always looking for what is no longer working, so that new ways can be created and implemented.

On the good ship organisation, on the high seas of continuous change, the leader is no longer the captain of the ship but the designer of the ship.

Always ready, willing and able to redesign or replace any system, process or task that is no longer efficient or effective.

Your flexibility is aligned with your creativity and your creativity is enhanced by your flexibility.

Question: What is the difference between efficiency and effectiveness and to what level is your team acheiving each? (1 is low 10 is high)

Reflection: It is more effective to involve others in the creation of new ways because...(list five reasons)

Action: List and review all current processes and tasks and assess each one for efficiency and effectiveness. (1 is low and 10 is high)

Pleasing Others

You are not concerned if you are 'pleasing' others or not, are you?

You know others will please themselves despite your behaviour, don't you?

You are never afraid to lose the approval of others, are you?

You are not beholden to others and are prepared to make and implement decisions that may not be popular, yes?

However, you are not insensitive to others 'sensitivities' and preferences.

You are careful to discern the emotional tendencies of each person's reactions.

You are always available to assist others to realise their own responsibility for their own thoughts and feelings.

But you are never afraid of other's reactions!

Question: Whose approval do you seek most?

Reflection: Why do you often worry about how others perceive you and feel about you – can you see the underlying cause?

Action: At the end of each day this week take five minutes to review the day. Ask yourself how differently you could have acted (visualise that behaviour) had you not been afraid of losing or not getting the approval of others.

Recognising People

The wise leader knows that humans are not resources.

To see another person as a 'resource' is to see them only as an object necessary to get a job done. It is to see their function before their humanity.

This 'people as resources' vision communicates itself to others and can subtly dehumanise them.

This is then reflected in the quality of energy exchanged in relationship, which eventual affects both the spirit and the cohesion of the team.

Every person is a person first, not an exploitable resource.

To build a community feeling as opposed to a corporate ethos requires connecting with others at a human level not just an efficient workforce.

That feeling then naturally influences levels of commitment and motivation.

Question: What kind of attitudes/behaviours do you currently display that may give the impression you see people as resources and not people?

Reflection: If you were to replace the term Human Resources what might be a more appropriate term?

Action: What three things could you do this week which demonstrates you care about the person first and their function/s in the task second?

Embracing Diversity

In the modern world diversity is not only a legal requirement in some countries, it's also an important, some would say vital, dimension of organisation and team building.

Diversity occurs at many levels including cultural conditioning, age, personality, race, belief systems, talent, creative capacity, relational tolerance and of course, gender!

A well-balanced team is usually a diverse team.

It has the voices of many perspectives from a variety of cultures and creative input from divergent mindsets.

To value diversity is to value people, to value people is to value diversity.

As you do, each person feels included and valued for what they uniquely bring to the team, however modest their contribution may sometimes be.

Question: How many levels of diversity do you have within your team?

Reflection: Why do you think diversity is often resisted? (can you find 3 reasons)

Action: Make a point of explicitly acknowledging and valuing diversity to each team member this week.

Results Responsibility

Making people responsible for results tends to enhance their level of commitment.

Even when that often means more work, perhaps more stress and pressure, yet it almost always causes commitment to increase.

The leader knows from their own experience that when people leave the meeting with no responsibility it results in a diminished level of commitment.

So why does responsibility for outcomes have such a positive influence? When given responsibility it says, "I trust you, I have confidence in you, I believe in your ability to deliver".

This stimulates a desire to prove one's self and return the leaders trust and faith.

The leader also knows "ownership" is closely tied to commitment. When people are given responsibility for making changes they're more committed to making the changes work.

Question: Do you find your self easily giving responsibility to others. If not, why do you think that is so?

Reflection: List all the reasons why delegating responsibility makes sense.

Action: Experiment this week with two members of your team by giving greater responsibility and watching what happens.

Grumpy Attacks

Sometimes it just feels like you got out of the wrong side of bed this morning.

You have a grumpy mood and everything in the day seems to be affirming that your grumpiness is accurate.

But how fast can you shake your self out of it?

If you don't then it will affect others around you. It may spread into the team. It may become a habit for you and also for everyone who looks to you for inspiration and guidance.

Changing a mood to order is not so easy. It's necessary to invent your own creative ways to break the spell.

Perhaps talking to someone who is always upbeat, taking a break and reading something humorous, perhaps reflecting on a recent mistake and deliberately seeking the funny side, perhaps laughing at your self for taking life so seriously.

Be creative as you find what works for you. In the meantime:

Scenario

FRED is highly critical of your management style.

He says things to others behind your back and whenever you speak to him he is moody and distant. You are upset by this and find it hard to communicate with him.

How would you handle this situation:

1 Internally within your self, within your own mind?

2 Externally in your interactions with Fred

3 How could you help Fred out of his habitual grumpiness?

Climate Change

There is a clear difference between the culture and the climate of the organisation.

Culture is rooted in the past traditions of the organisation which shape present-day routines, rituals and the 'the way we do things around here".

Climate, on the other hand, is the 'atmosphere now', which is what people perceive and 'feel' the way things are today.

You have less influence over a deeply embeded culture but a large influence over the immediate climate.

Can you see how your leadership style, based on your values, attitudes and priorities, have an instant impact on the day-to-day climate?

Can you see how your emotional state affects others?

As you set the tone and therefore the climate today, it has to have an impact on the culture over time.

Question: How would you describe the state of the climate in your organisation (dept/team) today?

Reflection: What are the key factors within your leadership style which is affecting the current climate?

Action: What do you need to adjust within your leadership style to enhance the current climate and what would that look like and feel like to others?

Empowering Creativity

While everyone appears to be motivated by different things one thing motivates all human beings and that's their own creativity.

The enlightened leader knows the secret formula:

I + O = C ...Involvement plus Ownership equals Commitment.

Whenever people are involved in the 'creation' of anything, from a plan to a process, a product to a procedure, they will have a greater sense of ownership and therefore a greater commitment to making it happen.

Whenever possible, refrain from imposing the plan or the process, in order to involve others in its creation.

While some may say they don't want to be involved in the creation of anything, find ways to facilitate small tastes of creative involvement.

Help people realise, "Yes I can make a creative contribution to this team".

By awakening them to their own creative spark you can progressively empower and motivate others through gradual involvement.

Question: Why do you think creativity is such a universal motivator?

Reflection: What blocks the creative impulse in people?

Action: Create three ways in which you could involve others more in the creative process of your work or role.

Your Vision

Effective communication is more to do with HOW something is said rather than with WHAT is said.

Even if the facts of what is said are true and for the benefit of the other, if it is said with any animosity it will not penetrate.

It will not connect with the other and will therefore not find acceptance in the other.

You already know that your communication is largely shaped by a combination of your vision/perception of your self and your vision/perception of the other.

If either vision/perception is negative in any way it will adversely influence the quality of your communication with everyone.

Question: How would you describe your vision of
a) yourself
b) each member of your team

Reflection: As is your vision so is your world! What does that mean?

Action: Consciously create a positive vision of each member of your team, regardless of any history, and allow it to influence your communication with them.

Brilliant Presentations

They say our greatest fear is public speaking.

Making a presentation to 6 people is often just as scary as 60 or 600, for some.

The ability to communicate clearly and inspiringly has long been recognized to be up there in the top four leadership competencies.

That's why, whenever you do, it makes sense to ask for others feedback, even have someone observe and critique you.

As you develop your ability in presenting it spills into all areas of your life.

Why? Life is relationship and relationship is built and sustained through communication.

It also enhances your self-confidence.

If there is one thing we never stop improving and fine-tuning it's our communication skills.

How to be a better communicator is always on the leaders 'to do' list.

Question: How have you improved your presentation skills during the last ten years?

Reflection: List what happens when you don't present well. List what happens when you do present well.

Action: Research and book yourself onto a presentations skills course, online or in-person. Then practice on your team. Ask for feedback, as well as being valuable, asking it's endearing.

Healing Fractures

The process of building collaborative relationships will likely trigger some conflict.

Relationship breakdown is often inevitable at some point.

Relations between team members is a crucial factor in the final outcomes of any group endeavour.

As is any form of 'communication breakdown' with each other or with the leader themselves.

Such 'breakdowns' are seldom terminal. They can always be repaired.

A carefully nurtured fracture in a relationship can be transformed into a point of strength for the future.

The repair will likely require a combination of honesty, vulnerability and humility - not necessarily in that order!

It makes sense therefore, to develop a high level of sensitivity to any signs of conflict.

Then, to be on hand to help heal such 'relationship fractures' either involving your self or between team members.

Question: Who are you currently experiencing a break down in relationship with, and who in the team is not connecting well with others?

Reflection: What do you think is the true cause of the break downs?

Action: What skills do you think you need to research and practice in order to heal broken relationships in the workplace - list, research and practice.

Creating Calm

The leader naturally senses their responsibility to stay calm at all times in order to show others how to create and sustain a calm atmosphere within the team.

When emotions run high, focus is lost and people are easily distracted by the dramas of others.

A tranquil setting is therefore an essential foundation to the process of empowering others to solve their own problems and co-create effective ways of working together.

Not being dependent on adrenaline shows others they can also work in a stress-free way.

This quietly helps the team to free themselves from their individual anxieties.

Anxiety only drains energy and serves as an accelerant towards exhaustion.

Being and staying calm in any crisis, helps everyone stay focussed yet relaxed, and able to enjoy what they do.

Question: How would you describe the atmosphere within your team on the following continuum – Tranquil = 1 Turbulent = 5 Emotional Chaos – 10

Reflection: Visualise what you would see happening differently if the setting/atmosphere were more tranquil (not passive).

Action: What three things could you do this week that would add to the tranquillity of the atmosphere?

Relational Power

The leader is aware of the difference between positional power and relational power. They will only use their positional power (if they have it) as a last resort.

They consciously build their relational power by respecting, trusting and genuinely caring for others.

Thus, enhancing their power of influence.

They know that leadership is dependent on retaining the respect and trust of others.

They never make the mistake of expecting to be respected.

Only some managers, who are not yet good leaders, 'expect' to be respected!

Enlightened leaders have liberated themselves from the lazy way to lead i.e. using positional power.

Question: What will happen eventually if you use positional power in workplace relationships – identify 3 possible outcomes!

Reflection: Write down the names of all your team members then assess your relationship (1 to 10) with each, where 1 indicates positional power being used, and 10 represents a relationship based on mutual respect and trust.

Action: Choose three people from those whom you lead and consciously build your relational power in the context of each relationship.

Position Less

Are you comfortable playing any role within a team?

Authentic leaders neither seek a position nor do they define themselves by their position.

They know that when you become 'position conscious', when your build your sense of 'who I am' out of a position, it is how the ego is created.

It's a mistake that leads to fear of loss, decisions skewed by the emotion of anxiety, behaviours that are compromised by the perceived need to 'protect my position'.

However, the leader understands that the culture and the protocols within the organisation often necessitate the official labelling of a position or a title.

But they don't use their position to define themselves. If they do then their self-esteem and self-confidence becomes statically tied to an idea.

They will then spend much energy looking for and defending against positional threats. Political games are likely to ensue.

Being positionless within your consciousness allows you to remain relaxed, flexibility and adaptable. This engenders a level of humility that attracts respect from team members.

Question: In what ways do you identify your self with your position.

Reflection: What emotions does this create within you?

Action: During the coming week create new ways to work alongside your team, as if you were another member of the team, each day.

Others Perspective

An effective leader has developed the ability to put themselves in the 'other's shoes'.

They can look through the eyes of the other, see what they see and get a sense of what they are feeling.

This ability to see the issue or situation from the others perspective provides several benefits, such as:

a) it generates a deeper understanding of 'the others' point of view

b) you are able to empathise to a greater degree with the feelings of 'the other'

c) you develop a deeper sense of where to begin guiding 'the other' to expand, focus or deepen 'the others' perspective … if necessary.

d) you can more effectively assist their colleagues to understand and align with that person

e) you learn new ways to see and interpret the issue/situation.

By being genuinely interested in and valuing the others perspective you also send the message 'I value you'.

Question: Whom, within your team, are you currently having difficulty in understanding?

Reflection: What inner preparation, within your consciousness, do you think you need to do to see clearly through the eyes of the other?

Action: Take a few moments each day this week to enquire into their perspective and look through their eyes by creating the best questions to commence your conversation.

Competition and Co-operation

There is always a dance between the polar opposites of competition and co-operation.

While building a culture of co-operation within the team you remain fully aware of the larger context, the marketplace.

The 'market' is founded and run on the ethos of competition.

The values and behaviors that arise from each are in opposition and therefore a possible cause of tension.

This means it's necessary to be continuously learning and improving your ability to foster one (co-operative teamwork) while operating in the other (competitive environment).

Gradually, through dialogue and discussion, you can teach and coach your team to identify, understand and resolve any tensions that arise around this clash of values and beliefs.

Question: Some say competition inevitably creates conflict? Would you say this is true? If so, why so? If not, why not?

Reflection: List the values and then the behaviors of competition against the values and behaviors of co-operation.

Action: Facilitate an open discussion with the team on the merits of competition and co-operation, exploring the benefits of each and the tensions between the two.

Perfection Release

As a leader, you would likely never 'insist' on perfection, unless it's a life or death situation, or legal issues are at stake.

You recognize the difference between what needs to be done accurately and what *just needs to get done.*

Unless, that is, you are an obsessively perfectionist person who is always tense and ready to jump at anything or anyone who does not meet your standards of perfection.

Your judgmental and critical perceptions only create tension within your self and then spread into the team.

The interpersonal atmosphere becomes edgy.

The wise leader has long since dropped the belief that 'everything' worth doing is worth doing perfectly in favour of *if it's worth doing then let's get it done ...well!*

The enlightened leader has realized there is no such thing as perfection!

Question: In what areas do you tend to be a perfectionist and why?

Reflection: What emotions do you tend to create around any need you have for perfection?

Action: This week practice less 'perfection control' and more 'encouraging continuous improvement'.

Opening Up

You understand the importance of team members communicating with each other.

Lines of communication are like arteries in the body carrying blood and oxygen to all corners of the body.

One of your key roles is connecting people with people and ensuring the blood and oxygen of information and experience flows smoothly round the network that is the team.

An ever-present priority is maintaining the efficiency of 'the network', ensuring any blockages and bottlenecks in the lines are 'fixed'.

Do people feel free and empowered to connect with others and are they aware how that benefits of both the task and the relationships?

Question: Where are the current blocks in the flow of communication within the team i.e. who is not talking to who and what is not being communicated where?

Reflection: What are the main causes for communication breakdown in your team?

Action: Note down what you think are the most effective ways to unblock and restore the flow of communication

Self Deprecation

The balanced leader has the capacity to laugh at themselves.

They take themselves lightly, at the 'appropriate' times.

They are not 'image conscious' and self-deprecation is expressed in the right place at the right moment ...in a natural way.

This trait within your character helps to put others at ease, especially those who have the tendency to place you, the leader, on a pedestal.

In being able to admit your own shortcomings you teach others, by example, that it's OK to be open and honest about themselves.

In being able to take your self lightly you keep the atmosphere relaxed and light, yet focussed and earnest, when required.

Question: On a scale of 1 to 10 (1 is low and ten is high)
a) how easily are you able to admit your faults?
b) how lightly do you take yourself?

Reflection: What do you think stops people from being able to take themselves lightly?

Action: Without forcing it, consciously practice the occasional moment of self-deprecation this week.

Eternal Optimist

There is always an upside to every apparent down turn, always some benefit in every event, regardless of how catastrophic it 'appears' to be.

You already know every cloud has a silver lining but it has to be consciously sought and identified.

With this grounded and stable perception, you are always able to look on the bright side, always able to 'find the positives' and therefore be heard and seen to be consistently optimistic.

At the same what needs to be fixed or changed is never ignored.

Your consistent optimism, in turn, brings a stable flow of enthusiastic energy that sustains the 'brightness' of the team.

Question: In what ways or in which situations could you be more optimistic? Why do we tend to find it so 'difficult' to discern 'the benefit' within every situation, see 'the positives' in every event?

Reflection: A wise old sage once said, "Nothing bad ever happens," - true or false, and why could this be true (reflect very deeply here!).
Review the past week or two and identify what apparently went wrong and then identify any hidden benefit/positives.

Action: Take five minutes each evening this week, review the day, and assess your levels of optimism during that day.

Support Circle

The intelligent leader sees and knows themselves as a support for others.

But they are wise enough to know they themselves also need to be supported.

Just as a trained counselor cannot counsel others until they themselves have been counseled, in the same way you will give greater support to others once you have been and are supported.

To this end cultivate your own set of supportive relationships, people with whom you can be fully open and revealing at all levels.

People you know will listen non-judgmentally, empathize and encourage you, in all that you do.

Through such relationships you learn what it feels like to be supported which then helps you to discern the best ways to support others.

Question: Who would you include in your group of supportive relationships?

Reflection: What difference does it make when you do not feel supported?

Action: Identify the exact nature of the support that you think each member of your team needs this week.

Agile Response

Being flexible, staying open, seeing the others view and practicing the art of detachment, are some of the prerequisite abilities necessary to practice agility.

Not a flexibility where anything goes.

But being able to bend when necessary to the needs of people and circumstances.

Not open to anything and everything.

But a degree of discernment that allows you to see what is appropriate or inappropriate in any given situation.

Not just blindly agreeing with others points of view.

But being able to assess and decide what is useful and what is not.

This requires the ability to become detached from one's own perspectives in order to appreciate different views.

Not detachment as in don't care or being cold. But the ability to stand back and see the bigger picture and not hold on tight to any position or personal perspective.

Question: What does being an 'agile' leader mean to you?

Reflection: As you look back on the people you have worked for or with, what were the memorable moments when you saw them being 'agile in action'?

Action: Ask your team for their thoughts on how you could be more agile. Allow the discussion to move in the direction of how the team itself could be more agile.

Collective Alignment

It's not a new idea that the direction of an organization, a team and an individual requires the alignment of three things - purpose, vision and values.

Purpose is what we are here to do.

Vision is a clear mental picture of how brilliantly our purpose is enacted.

Values are what shapes our decisions and behaviors on a day-to-day basis and that bring the purpose and vision into reality.

Is everyone in the team on the same page in terms of their awareness and understanding of these three components of life's rudder?

Is each individual continuously refreshing each component in their personal life?

The teams purpose, vision, values are then aligned to that of the organization.

When purpose is clear, direction becomes clear and energy is focussed.

It's usually a mistake to 'impose' the purpose and vision of the team. Whenever possible, work with the team to co-create both together.

Question: What is 'purpose' exactly? If asked about the purpose/vision/values of the organization would each member of the team give the same answer?

Reflection: It seems few people have a clear sense of purpose within the context of their work or their life, why do you think this is so? Reflect and discuss with some colleagues.

Action: Use a flip chart to 'refresh' the p/v/v of the team in a meeting this week.

Facing Up

Any problem or difficulty exists first and foremost within ones own consciousness.

The issue at hand is both external and internal as each person creates their own version of events and other peoples behaviors.

Only by facing up to ones inability to tolerate others is it possible to realise that it's not the other that is intolerable but ones own version of them that is intolerable.

Only by facing the fact that all stress is self created does one start to take responsibility for it's creation at the mental and emotional levels.

Only by facing up to ones own weaknesses can strength be built.

Otherwise much of our energy goes on supression and hiding.

The capacity to turn and face what is occuring within ones self is one of the foundations of being a leader.

Question: Why do you think we find it hard to see and face our own weaknesses?

Reflection: What happens within you when you avoid being responsible for your thoughts and feelings?

Action: Commence a discussion in this weeks team meeting around the question "What do you think we are not facing up to as a team and why?"

Subjective Objective

It's usually not a good idea to be subjective when interacting with or giving feedback to the members of the team.

Using judgmental and subjective adjectives such as "elusive," "secretive," "socially awkward," etc. tend to be alienating.

When you say things like, "I find you condescending", if you were to ask five people what a "condescending employee" is there will likely be five explanations that are NOT identical.

We all have different perceptions with which we create different realities. When judgmental adjectives are being used it's not about the other person anymore, it's more about our self.

The enlightened leader is more objective and describes the behavior as, "He often interrupts others in the meeting while they are talking with him", and, "He almost never listens to others when they try to give him feedback"

Describing behaviors which are observable, measurable and specific, allow you to give specific feedback – whether it is positive feedback or constructive feedback.

Focus on behavior, ensure 'they' understand what you mean and try to ask, ask, ask, as much as possible.

Question: Review the last three times you gave some feedback - what percentage was subjective and what percentage objective

Reflection: How do you feel when you perceive others judging you?

Action: Write a list of your team members and decide what kind of objective feedback would be good for each.

Troubled Negaholic

When you are in the presence of someone who is always looking darkly at people and situations it's often difficult not to be influenced by their negativity.

We color each other by the quality of our company.

Seeing the downside of an event, perceiving the weakness in others, creating negative thoughts, all become habits by which we sabotage our self first and foremost.

If there are any battlegrounds in life it has to be within our self as we seek to release such habits and replace them with the ability to remain upbeat, optimistic and with the ability to look on the bright side of, well, everything.

As you do you notice an increase in your ability to be around the negaholic and to color them with brighter attitudes, perceptions and thoughts.

Yes, it sounds obvious, perhaps even simple, but unfortunately some of us have simply grown up with darker influences in our life.

Scenario

DAVID is someone who likes to create a scene, is frequently negative and always trying to upset others.

He is seen by the rest of the team as 'the problem', as a trouble maker. Everyone else tends to complain about him. But he has also shown moments of brightness and has good ideas. It's his attitude that often puts people off.

How would you handle this situation?

> 1 Internally within your self
>
> 2 Externally in your personal interactions with David
>
> 3 Externally in your interactions with the rest of the team who also find David a 'killjoy' in so many ways.'

Individualism and Community

There is a balance between the individual and the collective.

The predominant cultural context is often biased towards one or the other.

In some countries, individualistic tendencies are strong.

There is little sense of teamwork and community.

This can act against the cultivation of an effective team.

In other cultures, the family unit is still predominant.

There, the urge towards community can be too strong, giving rise to over familiarity and a lack of focus on the task.

When you notice this kind of bias you can then put strategies in place to correct the balance so that both the individual and the team flourish.

Question: How would you describe the balance between individual and community, within your team (ask the team also)?

Reflection: Why do you think the balance is biased one way, towards the individual, or another, towards community?

Action: What could you do to redress the balance?

Pick Practices

The enlightened leader knows they can develop any skill, ability, propensity, inclination and intention.

It requires only that 'attention' is given to the selected attribute.

The principle is: Where your attention goes, energy flows and where your energy flows, things grow.

If the actual skill/ability etc. is known only by name and not understood in any depth, then some research may be required.

First naming, then understanding, then experimentation and then implementation, until there is integration,

Only then does that skill/ability become a part of one's repertoire.

The starting point is a simple list.

Question: What would be the top twenty leadership attributes, qualities, characteristics you would like to add to your personal leadership 'competency profile'? Write a list.

Reflection: Pick one at a time. Research it using Google and Amazon. Study it. Get under the skin of this particular attribute and find the wisest voices 'out there' on each one.
Ask your self, "What stops me being able to enact this skill/attribute"?

Action: Identify. Research. Experiment. Practice. Enact. Implement. Integrate.

Employee Inclinations

The workplace often has two types of employees – the committed and the engaged.

Engaged employees are those who go the extra mile, beyond what is required.

They are the ones who give their discretionary effort to their work on a consistent basis.

Committed employees are those who trust you, respect you. They would follow you even if you went to work for a different company.

Some may be highly engaged within their work but not committed to you.

They could easily go to work for somebody else.

Others may be committed employees but not very engaged with their work.

The leader senses the levels to which each employee is engaged and committed, and allows that assessment to influence the way they relate, empower and coach each member of their team.

Question: Would you say you are committed or engaged, or both? If both, what would be the percentage of each?

Reflection: Why do you think some employees are more engaged than committed and vice versa?

Action: Write a list of all your direct reports and assess each one by giving a percentage 'engaged' and percentage 'committed'.

Leadership Competency

Are leaders born or made?

They say any competency, hard or soft, is made up of three ingredients: knowledge, skill and aptitude.

Knowledge: You may have all the knowledge in the world about guitar playing. But if you never touch a guitar – you will not be able to play it.

Skill: You may have the skill to play the guitar because you have played it since you were a child. But if you cannot read musical notes, if you don't know the theory of music, if you don't know about guitar composition, you probably won't be able to play it very well.

Aptitude: You may practice playing guitar and study guitar theory, the same number of hours as John Williams did. You may even become a pretty good guitar player – but you will never play the guitar as John Williams does.

Leaders are born – and – leaders are made.

Question: As you reflect on your leadership competency which of the above three areas is your strongest and which is your weakest.

Reflection: What do think you need to do in each area to enhance your competency.

Action: Identify someone you know who is competent in each area or in all three areas and spend some time with them this week curiously exploring what they have done to enable themselves to become competent.

Role Sharing

While you may have accepted the leadership role there are times and situations when it's good to relinquish the role.

If only temporarily, so others may assume the role.

If one person is always seen to be deciding and directing, others easily feel they are simply an extension of that person.

The wise leader knows when to 'share the burden' before they themselves feel over burdened or overwhelmed by the demands of solitary leadership.

In sharing the burden of leadership, they are also calling forth the potential of others.

In sharing the burden of leadership, they demonstrate they are not attached to, and dependent on, the role.

In sharing the burden of leadership, they show they are not using the role to mistakenly define themselves.

Question: On a scale of one to ten how attached are you to being the leader/doer/initiator all the time (1 is low and 10 is high)

Reflection: Why do most leaders not share the burden of leadership with others – list five reasons.

Action: Who in your team do you see as potential leaders with whom you can share your burden occasionally? Create a list of responsibilities that you could share on a progressive scale. Create a rough plan to share...progressively.

Behind Appearances

Things are seldom what they appear to be.

Symbols, known as words, can only 'point' to a deeper meaning, not capture meaning itself. The meaning of these words is created by you.

Similarly, the behaviors of others are only symbolic of underlying attitudes and emotional states.

Someone who is always critical of others (attacking) is disguising a state of fear within themselves.

Never take anything at 'face value' i.e. literally. Learn and cultivate the ability to interpret the 'behavioral symbols' that are occurring around you.

In time, and with 'reading practice', you will develop the finer arts of discerning the deeper meaning of others attitudes and actions.

However, such practice needs to be consciously chosen and frequent, without judgment and with the intention to genuinely understand and the other.

Question: Why is it not healthy to interpret everything literally?

Reflection: While on the surface someone's negative behavior appears to sabotage the team what do you sense is really going on behind that behavior and what is really going on behind the reactions of the other members of the team?

Action: Select three members of your team this week and have a chat with them in which your aim is to discern what is the true underlying mental/emotional cause of their behavior.

Change Management

In the context of an exponentially changing world a certain term known as VUCA has entered the corporate lexicon.

As an acronym for **V**olatility, **U**ncertainty, **C**omplexity and **A**mbiguity it describes the characteristics of change.

However, before you can assist your team to understand and effectively manage these characteristics they must first manage them within themselves.

Volatility: At a personal level a volatile consciousness means emotional reactions are increasing. The leader is always deepening their emotional intelligence so they can 'respond' more and 'react' less.

Ambiguity: With the understanding that we are each a 'maker of meaning' the leader is continuously refining their intellect in order to bring clarity of perception and depth of understanding to both external and internal issues.

Complexity: In a world of technological expansion and sophistication the leader always attempts to bring issues and concerns back to the essence with the intention and mantra 'how can we simplify this'.

Uncertainty: With the awareness that there is nothing more certain than increasing uncertainty, the leader is prepared for all eventualities and is never surprised or shocked by any unpredicted events.

Question: Which of the above do you think *you* and *your team* face the most?

Reflection: How could you equip and empower your team to handle each area more effectively?

Action: Introduce your team to VACU and initiate a discussion within the team to explore the impact of each aspect on their work.

Difficult Behaviors

Everyone seems to have a difficult person in their life. Someone who just seems to press all the wrong buttons to ensure we react and temporarily lose our ability to consciously and creatively respond.

But there is no such thing as a difficult person, if you so decide.

It's not the person that is difficult, it's your 'version' of them.

That's why some people seem difficult for some but not for others.

It's our perception that creates them and labels them as difficult.

If we do that twice then it's likely to become an automatic habit within our consciousness.

In a sense, they become our master. Because we 'react' to them they become the leader in the relationship.

The enlightened leader knows this and can show how not to be affected by the words, attitudes and behaviors of others.

The wisest leaders are always working on reducing their 'reactivity'!

They are careful not to create a version of the other that they label 'difficult'!

Question: Identify the two most challenging relationships out of all the people that you know.

Reflection: Why do you think they can be difficult relationships for you.

Action: Deliberately interact as much as possible with those two people this week. But with the aim of making the relationship, easier, smoother. Try different strategies.

Advocating Inquiry

As the leader engages in meaningful conversations they balance advocacy with inquiry. Advocacy is when you promote your own ideas. Advocacy is when you try to proactively influence the other person.

Advocacy is when you champion your point of view to effectively sell your perspectives, concepts, suggestions, etc.

However, advocacy is wisely balanced with the practice of 'inquiry'.

Inquiry is when you genuinely try to understand before trying to be understood. Inquiry is when you receptively listen to the opposing ideas/argument.

Inquiry is used in coaching – where the coach wants to gain a deeper understanding about the 'others' behaviors, context, reasons, etc., to better help him or emerge their full potential.

Many leaders ignore the potential of inquiry.

The enlightened leader asks their team to start practicing both, thereby enhancing the quality of the team's discussions and decisions.

Question: In what proportion do you personally tend to use advocacy versus enquiry (e.g. 60/40)?

Reflection: Why do you think you lean towards one and not balance well with the other? What might it add to your relationships if you sought a greater balance?

Action: In three specific relationships this week consciously practice a balanced approach between advocacy and inquiry.

Forbid Formality

Formality can often be the worst enemy of the leader as it tends to inhibit openness and honesty amongst the team.

When the leader needs an accurate perspective, honest input and authentic opinions to resolve problems within the team, it is often the rigid observance of convention or manners that ensures formality will get in the way of truth-telling.

Without the truth being told, it's often impossible to make the best possible decision.

Formality can encourage employees to suppress their self-expression as they don't speak up and withhold their feedback. This one way they can avoid conflict.

A formal environment is not conducive to clear communication as it's not fully open. The leader is responsible for creating and sustaining such a formal environment.

If the leader wants to constantly create breakthrough ideas it's necessary to create an environment that allows for a smooth flow of ideas, open conversations, constructive use of conflict and many moments of informal engagement between members of the team and the leader.

Question: How would you go about creating a less formal environment in your organization or team?

Reflection: In what ways does formality often get in the way of the effectiveness of your team and your relationships within the team?

Action: Create ways to role model less formality, talk about it, teach its value, praise it, and most of all, find ways to reward it.

Delegate Power

Powerlessness can easily produce despair, a "What's the use?" attitude, that stifles enthusiasm and saps energy.

The enlightened leader endeavours to give each employee some control and authority over some area of work.

They share the power.

They delegate authority.

They are always looking for ways to allow everyone to take charge of something.

People, as individuals, then feel they have some influence over ideas and events.

The aim? To prevent people feeling powerless as it diminishes commitment.

Even a small amount of power may keep an employee from giving up and disengaging.

The leader knows they can give power to their people without ending up any less powerful themselves.

Question: Think of a time when you had absolutely no authority over anything - how did you feel?

Reflection: Think of three good reasons to give people more authority in the work/task/process of the team.

Action: Make a list of your team members and identify in what ways you could delegate power/responsibility to each one.

Tuning and Timing

You are a conductor.

Before you is an orchestra of many musicians with their instruments, in the form the skills, talents, qualities and strengths. All contained within the members of your team

As a conductor, your role is to ensure the instruments play the right note at the right time in the right place at the right tempo.

To that end, you ensure the musicians are guided to play the same melody together, listening for any instrument that is slightly out of tune and letting that musician know they have some fine-tuning to do.

As the conductor, you set the rhythm of the music, raising and lowering the volume and the tempo when the symphony requires it.

As the conductor, you also know there is a time to rehearse, a time to tune up, a time to perform and a time to rest ...a little!

Question: How would you describe the symphony that you, as a leader, are conducting and the tempo at which it needs to be played?

Reflection: Your vision is their sheet music… why?

Action: Create a seating plan (on paper) for your orchestra (team) identifying the person and the talents/skills, whom each needs to sit next to, and with whom they need to harmonise most.

Belonging Inside

Are you aware of those who show up for work every morning but don't feel they 'belong' to the organization?

Are you aware of people on the inside who feel like outsiders?

Do you give time and attention to identifying those who don't feel included, those who perhaps have not been allowed into heart of the organization?

People who feel excluded often put in nothing more than their time.

Employees who feel left out or ignored tend to invest less enthusiasm in their work.

The leader pulls every person in, drawing people together and includes everyone in the communication loop.

The leader knows that to feel accepted, time and attention is needs to be given, to different degrees, to each member of the team.

People often need to feel they belong, until they don't feel the need to belong!

Question: What are the main reasons why people may feel outsiders in your organisation/team?

Reflection: To what extent do you feel like you belong, that you are included, that you are an insider? What difference does it make to your motivation?

Question: List your team members and then consider to what percentage you sense each has a sense of belonging. If necessary, ask them.

Conflict Dissolution

Conflict within a group is as predictable as the sunrise.

Working together means a clash of egos will, at some stage, interfere with the harmony, balance and focus of the team.

When it happens it's never useful to take sides, no matter how right one side appears to be. Nor is it ever helpful to accuse either party, no matter how wrong one side appears to be.

Wisdom says facilitate the awareness of each party towards the realisation of their contribution to the conflict. So that each has a full awareness of their attachment to their position/opinion/view.

Then, to help each understand the position of the other.
In so doing each side sees their contribution to the conflict while understanding the 'other'.

Only when each side can 'dissolve' their part of the conflict, even temporarily, can the journey to resolution begin.

Thus, the leader learns to be a coach, a guide, a teacher and a facilitator at the same time.

Question: Where in your team/group do you currently discern conflict - between which two parties?

Reflection: What is the deepest reason/cause of conflict that is common to all conflicted relationships?

Action: Create three questions that you would ask each party within a current conflict that may help each side become more aware of their contribution to the conflict.

Leaders Humility

You may be a manager, but If you 'think' you are 'the leader' you're probably not! Why? Because you've created an idea, perhaps an image, of your self as the leader and you become attached to, and identified with, that idea in your own mind.

There will inevitably be moments when someone decides not to follow, or someone criticises what you have said or done, or someone is obviously more positive in their attitude than you.

These are moments when you can sense, deep down, that you are not living up to your 'ideal'. Or others are not recognising your 'ideal'.

In all such moments, you will likely lose your internal stability and certainly your humility. This will affect your decision making, your ability to interact sensitively and proactively.

Thereby diminishing your effectiveness as a leader.

That's why the enlightened leader doesn't consider themselves as 'the leader'. They don't build an 'ego' out of the idea or an image of themselves as leader.

They remain free internally to be and do what authentic leaders do, which is help, guide, encourage, influence, respect, trust, counsel …the list goes on. But they 'be and do' this without the loss of internal stability or the tension that comes from holding on to the idea 'I am the leader'.

Question: Do you have an image or idea of your self as 'the' leader?

Reflection: What do you feel when you think of your self as 'the' leader.

Action: Practice dropping the idea of being a leader and see how it feels and how it changes the energy you give to others.

Creative Destruction

You are aware that destruction is necessary not just to survive but to thrive, develop and grow.

Just as a snake sheds a skin it has outgrown, the organisation, the team and individuals, often need to destroy old habits, patterns and processes that have outlived their usefulness.

Perhaps it's doing away with bureaucratic practices, or breaking with traditions when they become obstacles.

Perhaps it's challenging the stubborn protection of old beliefs, or it's just getting rid of outmoded work practices.

The leader is always vigilant to see what practices are no longer serving the team and is not afraid to change them or end them.

Even though it may get messy and some people may become upset, only when the old is cast aside can the new be nurtured and allowed to flourish.

The leader knows that for organizations, teams and individuals to stay strong and relevant, sacrifices must be made, sometimes occasionally, sometimes frequently.

Question: What old patterns, habits or bureaucratic practices do you perceive to be obstacles to development and progress. Make a list for the team, the organisation and your self!

Reflection: What might the updated and nurtured 'new ways' look like.

Action: Initiate a 'renewal conversation' with the team this coming week with the question, "What do we need to sacrifice in order to develop and move forward"?

Practice Perfect

They say practice makes perfect. Perhaps! But it's noticeable that nobody suggests there can real improvement without practice.

The leader is aware that team performance improvements are not possible without regular, structured practice.

Improvement is seldom achieved by merely 'doing the job' or just 'playing the game.'

Practice gives the team a chance to focus solely on performance, without having to worry about results at the same time. The team experiments and makes mistakes, then creates corrections.

When difficulties are found, they try new ways, work on new routines and perhaps do things they couldn't afford to do if it were in a 'real life' situation.

Practice develops that 'edge' that allows them to outperform the competition.

Practice allows them to learn how to anticipate the challenges of previously unanticipated problems that might occur.

Question: What are the aspects of your teams work that could be 'practiced' in order to improve? Identify three areas.

Reflection: What would 'practicing' each of the three look like?

Action: Ask the team what they think would be valuable processes, methods and techniques to practice as a team.

Conversational Connections

Globalization, new technologies, the 'gig economy' and innovative ways to enhance customer value, have all radically changed the communications landscape within organisations.

The management approach that has served us for the last hundred years i.e. the top down model of command and control, is dying fast.

Traditional corporate communications are giving way to a process that is more dynamic, creative and inclusive. That process is conversational.

The leader's engagement with employees is more like an ordinary person-to-person conversation than someone issuing directives from on high.

Creative conversations where the leader co-creates new ideas with employees; *informational conversations* where there is a reciprocal exchange of essential information; *problem solving conversations* where a mutual search seeks ways to solve difficult issues; *conflict resolving conversations* where the leader consults the conflicted parties on the best routes to resolution.

These kinds of conversation not only seek and value the input of everyone, but connect people in ways that starts to look more like a small family unit than it does a large formal organisation.

Question: What percentage of current exchanges with your team are genuinely conversational i.e. two way exchanges?

Reflection: To what extent do you facilitate and truly listen to each member of your team – make a mental list of people and assess your self in each relationship.

Action: Focus on practicing and refining your conversational skills with each member of the team during this coming week.

Eliminate Blame

Most of us have developed what seems to be a natural bias to 'blame' someone when things don't go to plan.

This bias can be corrected by practicing your own version of DRAW which stands for Don't - Review - Ask - Work.

Don't blame; assume that the performer had the best of intentions.

Review the possible reasons, related to their efforts, that may explain the lack of performance.

Ask them what happened, making sure you ask with the tone that is genuinely assuming their intentions were good.

Work together, and co-create strategies to fix any performance problems, ensuring it won't occur in the future.

Suggestion: Pin DRAW to the office noticeboard and allow it to spread.

Question: When was the last time you 'blamed' or 'criticized' a team member for their performance?

Reflection: Use that memory to construct a different non-blaming response (DRAW) as if you were going through the same situation.

Action: Find two instances in the coming week when you practice your version of DRAW.

Bossy Boss

Sometimes, when people are elevated into a leadership position they start to become quite authoritarian. A combination of their own insecurities, the demands of the job and their effort to 'do well', come to the surface and their personality becomes more forceful and, well, bossy!

Are you a bossy boss? Do you have a bossy boss?

After many workshops and seminars on many topics that involve self-change, leadership development and management strategies, perhaps you've come away with much wisdom and many tips and techniques, but still your character, your approach, has stayed almost the same.

Fixed in your ways it's not easy to change style and change the way you relate to other people.

It's one reason why 'learning driven' change has to come from inside out and not outside in. When it does it doesn't take long to realize that if one is to change one's character and its habitual behaviors it's more about unlearning than learning.

In the meantime, how would you respond to this scenario?

Scenario

Your `boss' is struggling with his leadership style. He is a strong character and although he talks about empowering, motivating and influencing, he still uses positional power (command and control) to get things done. He is a bossy boss!

Sometimes he tries to soften his approach but it's clear he gets impatient. Being more flexible and open is obviously difficult for him. He has also been on a variety of self-management courses where you know he has been learning how to see himself differently and pick up some relationship skills.

1 What do you think could be the underlying 'issue' (blockage) with your boss?

2 In what ways could you help your boss to soften his style?

Power Shifts

Have you made the shift from force to power?

Have you realised you cannot control others (force) and learned to influence (empower)?

Have you ceased to see others as objects/resources to get the job done (force) and now see others as human beings (empower) with whom the relationship is more important than the task?

Have you ceased to compete with others (force) and hold out the hand of co-operation to everyone (empower)?

Have you cultivated the trait of asking before telling?

Have you separated your beliefs from your values?

Have you decided 'why' you are here, to survive or to serve?

Question: Why do we attempt to force by trying to control others? What are the main signs when someone else is trying to force you?

Reflection: Identify three other shifts you could make from force to power?

Action: Each day for the next week visualise one situation you know that you will face during the day and see yourself acting from your power and not attempting to force.

Intuitive Intelligence

Wisdom arises from cultivating the capacity to listen to one's own subtle feelings.

For many this is not easy as we tend to grow up and be conditioned within a context that emphasizes rationality before intuition.

We tend to prefer to want to think things through and thereby delay decisions and actions. Sometimes this is appropriate.

Becoming sensitive to our subtler feelings requires regular practice of some form of reflection or contemplation, even meditation.

At such times memories, thoughts and mental stories are put to one side and a deeper awareness of what lies beyond the mind, prior to mental activity, is cultivated.

It is here that the wisdom of the heart is accessed. A wisdom that arises as feelings, not thoughts. Feelings that have no rationality to back them up until, perhaps, after they've been translated into action.

Choosing a journey route can be intuitive. Choosing the person and the best moment to delegate a task can be intuitive. As can how much to say to someone when they have made a mistake.

The more you cultivate and use your intuition the more accurate it becomes and the more it can be trusted.

Question: What does intuition mean to you and when in the past have you allowed your self to be guided by it?

Reflection: Pick an issue/situation you are currently facing, sit with it quietly in your mind, then watch your feelings.

Action: As you talk to each person on your team this week consciously practice being aware of your feelings during the conversation.

Performance Boost

The progressive leader is always seeking ways to improve performance.

They frequently bring the team together to brainstorm ideas to increase their collective effectiveness.

The only requirement is a flip chart, perhaps a set of post-it notes and the whole team in one room for a couple of hours.

Ideas are the currency and the best facilitator is chosen to lead the first part of the brainstorming session.

> a) Initially focusing on quantity of ideas - not quality - divergent thinking is essential.
>
> b) All ideas are valid - especially the most unusual ones.
>
> c) Integrating and improving ideas, stealing and growing other's ideas, seeking the connections between ideas, are all encouraged.
>
> d) Criticism is discouraged to ensure the group energy remains creative and dynamic.

The second part of the session is the evaluation and elimination stage as each idea is evaluated by the team, allowing the cream to rise to the top!

Question: Why would you want your team to work together to find new ways to work together?

Reflection: What other benefits are hidden in a team brainstorming session?

Action: Call the team together in the next two weeks and if you know someone on the team who is already a good facilitator ask them to facilitate at least a part of the sessions.

Leaders Perception

The old-style manager has the tendency to concentrate on others weaknesses rather than their strengths.

They tend to focus on what's going wrong more than what's going well.

Their negative attitude often makes them pessimists who see the difficulty in every opportunity rather than the opportunity in every difficulty.

The enlightened leader, on the other hand, acknowledges what's not gone well, but quickly moves to correct, learn any relevant lessons, and then move on.

They always look for the positives, seeing the strengths of others, in any situation while radiating a consistently optimistic attitude.

A seven point checklist as you reflect on the day just gone - were you upbeat, optimistic, strength focussed, proactive, solution orientated, inclusive and caring.

Marks out of ten for each?

Question: Why do you think we 'tend' to see the weaknessess of others before their strengths?

Reflection: What you see is what you are! Why might this be so?

Action: Write down the names of five people who work for you and then identify the three key strengths of each person.

Self Responsibility

One belief sabotages your ability to influence others and thereby empower others.

It's the belief that, "It's not me, it's them, that makes me feel this way".

This belief underlies the projection of responsibility onto others and the avoidance of self-responsibility.

If you do not accept self-responsibility you are dis-empowering your self.

So when you say, "I am here to empower you", they are unlikely to take you seriously.

To point the finger at others or circumstance is to develop a 'victim mindset'.

In such moments, you lose your credibility in their eyes.

Accepting total responsibility for one's thoughts, feelings, actions, in every situation and in every relationship, regardless of the nature of the event, the circumstances or the insult, is to signify your return to self-mastery.

It also sets a brilliant example.

Question: Who are two people you tend to project responsibility for your feelings at most frequently and for what?

Reflection: What is the underlying reason that we project responsibility onto others for anything? (use a real life past experience and create a trail of questions before you answer)

Action: In your next encounter/s with the person/s onto whom you tend to project responsibility for what you feel interrupt the pattern by seeking a deeper understanding of the other.

Good Feedback

The 'leader as coach' is acutely aware of the power and effect of giving frequent feedback.

They know that just the tone of their communication can have the effect of encouraging or alienating.

They are also aware that the relevance and timing can also affect how the feedback will be received in the minds of others.

The aware leader takes the time to 'sense' the capacity of each member of their team to both receive feedback and to use that feedback to change the way they operate.

Be not afraid to give your feedback.

The more you practice giving it the easier it becomes and the more it is then expected and desired.

Without feedback, seldom does change happen for the better.

Question: What works for you most effectively when you give feedback? And what doesn't work?

Reflection: Why do you avoid giving feedback to some people and not to others and how would you change that?

Action: Each day this week identify whom you need to consciously give feedback and exactly how you will approach it.

Psychological Safety

At Google, they did a study of teamwork. They wanted to know what makes the most effective team.

It wasn't the team with the most technical or functional expertise. It wasn't about cognitive capability. It was about psychological safety.

People felt comfortable when they had a sense that they could succeed or fail and that they would still be supported by their colleagues on the team. That they wouldn't be criticised, judged or blamed. That there would be a constructive outcome to whatever it was that happened. Failure would result in learning and discussion, recalibrating and another attempt.

But the critical thing was knowing how to put psychological safety into effect.

It's an interpersonal process that primarily has to do with non-cognitive intelligence.

It's built out of understanding the other, compassion, empathy and care.

The sense of psychological safety occurs when people 'feel' themselves to be in a 'culture of care'.

Question: What behaviours do you demonstrate that shows you care about each member of the team as a human being. List.

Reflection: How did you feel when someone cared about you and was non-judgmental and empathic towards you.

Action: List the people who work for you and with you and decide how you can connect with more personal 'care' towards each one this week.

Curing Problemitis!

The leader cannot afford to catch one of the world's most popular
dis-eases, known as problemitis!

Change does throw up many challenges and obstacles, blocks
and barriers, but leadership requires sharpness of perception and
an attitude that refuses to be influenced by the pessimists and the
negaholics.

It's maybe a cliché to say, "There are no problems only
opportunities", but in reality, the actual switch in perception is
harder to make than simply reiterating such a popular aphorism.

It begins with 'possibility thinking'. By installing the habit of
always creating new and innovative ways to get work done then,
when barriers do appear, such a habit immediately triggers a
creative search for ways round, over, under.

This kind of response to apparent problems and obstacles is
enhanced by creative conversations. That's when the leader
opens the floor to everyone's ideas so frequently that people start
thinking creatively long before any meeting commences.

They start to look forward meetings and arrive with new ideas
ready-made.

Question: When was the last time you consciously decided to
use a problem as an opportunity to improve something?

Reflection: What current troubles at work contain some kind of
opportunity?

Action: Write down the names of your team in a list. Then rate
each one where 1 is low and 10 is high, as a) someone who gets
stuck in the problem and then b) as someone who is upbeat and
seeking creative solutions. In the meeting ask the one with the
lowest score for their ideas first.

Incognito Leader

Shun the limelight.

Seek no recognition for your character.

But if it comes accept it with grace and move on.

Seek no applause for results.

But if it comes accept it with humility and move on.

Seek no reward for your endeavours.

But if it comes accept it and share it as much as possible.

Seek not to glorify your self, but in the wise words of Lao Tzu:

Go to the people
Live amongst them
Start with what they have
Build on what they know
And when the deed is done,
The mission accomplished
Of the best leaders
The people will say,
'We have done it ourselves'

Question: What happens when you seek recognition or affirmation of your role as a leader a) within your self and b) in your relationship with others?

Reflection: Why does any human being crave the recognition of others – what might it signify?

Action: This week make a conscious effort to allow others to receive the credit.

Non-Judgmental

To judge another creates a subtle barrier in the relationship.

Being judged by someone has two dimensions. Evaluation of the action and judgement of the person.

When a person is judged it can easily trigger a closing of their mind. Not cause, but trigger. Especially if they have been harshly judged by parents or friends as children. These were the moments when we created the habit of going into ourselves and, as they did, they created the habit of suppressing their energy.

Evaluation of someone's action is essential if you are to give effective feedback and improve performance.

But it's a fine line between 'evaluation of action' relevant to getting the job done well and 'judgement of behavior' as a result of that behavior triggering your own discomfort.

Take nothing 'personally'. This allows you to remain unbiased and present to help, nurture, care and coach the other.

Question: What's the difference between coaching someone to improve their behavior and reacting judgmentally to someone's behavior.

Reflection: Take a moment to reflect on your interactions over the last week and see if you can find moments when you 'judged' the person instead of solely evaluating their performance.

Action: Watch for at least three opportunities this week to consciously evaluate someone's performance and then giving non-judgmental feedback.

Purpose First

Everything has a purpose.

Every task, process and meeting will only work efficiently and effectively if it's 'on purpose'. In other words, only when purpose is clear will energy, ideas, thoughts and actions be generated and used in the most efficient and effective way.

However, purpose is often forgotten. It is often missed as the laziness and comfort zone of habit kicks in.

Sometimes meetings become automatic rituals – things we do because we've always done them.

Sometimes the process is way out of date because no one asked, "Is this process still 'fit for purpose'?

Sometimes tasks that were vital last year are no longer necessary because they no longer serve the larger purpose.

With any task or process start with the question of purpose. Frequently review the task/process to make sure it's still focused by the same purpose. Then evaluate everything according to how well it served the overall purpose.

Why are you/we doing this? Why are you/we working here and not there? Are challenging questions that invite people to refresh, if not discover, their personal purpose. And, as the old saying goes, if you don't live your life 'on purpose' you will live your life by accident!

Question: Make a list of all the processes and tasks you and your team are involved in creating and sustaining.

Reflection: Look at each process/task and ask your self, and perhaps the whole team, is our purpose clear with regards to this process/task.

Action: In consultation with the team trim any activities that are not relevant, expand those that are, where appropriate.

Detached Involvement

While detachment can be mistaken for uncaring or coldness or avoidance, it is an essential leadership practice.

When you are attached to people then what happens to them feels like it's happening to you.

If individuals or the team are feeling shocked you will be shocked, if they are feeling disappointed at failing, you will feel the same way, if they are raging against some changes in the organisation you will likely rage with them. This is attachment.

The more enlightened leader will do almost the opposite. They will stay cool and unaffected by the situation or by others reactivity.

They will remain detached but engaged. They remain fully involved but not at the emotional level.

Otherwise they lose their focus and clarity. Others notice how easily they become unstable and then respect is lost.

Detached involvement means being fully present to listen, guide, advise and facilitate, while being unaffected by the emotional dramas of others, regardless of the event or situation that is occurring.

Easy theory, but not so easy to practice.

Question: When was the last time you faced a crisis within your team - either collectively or individually? What was their reaction and what was your response?

Reflection: Being calm and cool in heated situations means ceasing to become emotional! True or false? If so why so?

Action: Open a discussion this week with the team asking the questions: a) what is the meaning and benefits of detached involvement and b) how do you do it?

Task Relationship

What comes first, the task or the relationship?

Ask most managers and they will say the task. Ask most leaders and they will say relationship. Watch their behaviours and it's probably true to say that most will put the task before the relationship.

After all, we go to work to do a task, not build relationships.

There are deadlines for tasks which focus our attention but there are no deadlines for relationships. The customer is not so interested about how we are all getting along. They just want their product or service pronto and of a high quality.

This is why, as a leader, it's often necessary to remind your self each day your first priority is people. You lead people not tasks or processes.

Your task is the get the tasks done through people!

Building relationships, talking to people, resolving conflicts, noticing individual needs, then become the main areas of focus.

Happy people do their best work.

Harmonious relationships get work done efficiently and effectively.

Obviously, but life conditions us to focus first on the task and that often gets in the way.

Question: What are the reasons you tend to focus on the task more than people?

Reflection: The leaders task is people - what does that mean exactly?

Action: At the end of each day this coming week ask yourself this question: In what ways did I focus on people today? Note down in your journal.

Time In

Each situation and each relationship is different, requiring a different but appropriate response. Obviously.

However, responses are not subject to an academic standard or formulaic procedure.

They require a clear intellect that can discern exactly what is happening.

An uncluttered mind that can freely focus on the moment and allow a smooth flow from perception to thought to action.

Without the influence of baggage (experience and beliefs) from the past.

This is why there is huge value in giving regular time to cleaning/clearing the mind and sharpening the intellect.

Only then can you increase your ability to discern, decide and respond according to the needs of the person/situation in front of you.

Question: Why do you sometimes find it hard to discern and decide what is the best way to respond to someone or the best thing to do in certain circumstances?

Reflection: Review a recent challenging interaction or situation in which you had to respond quickly and assertively. What might you do differently in hindsight?

Action: Take time out each day this week to reflect, review and self-assess the appropriateness, wisdom and general quality of your responses during that day.

Empathic Connection

It's often not so easy to empathize, especially after a lifetime of learning to sympathize.

Step one is knowing the difference between apathy, sympathy and empathy.

APATHY means "I don't care what your feeling or about the predicament you are in". SYMPATHY sounds like "Oh what a shame, how sad, I feel terrible for you". EMPATHY is more like, "Tell me what you're feeling and why you think you feel that way".

The leader knows that empathy means being sensitive to the feelings of the other without creating the same emotional state within one's self.

Building an empathic relationship requires patient listening skills and a sincere interest in what exactly the other person is feeling and why.

Once this level of exchange is created between two people the relationship tends to become lastingly solid and eventually one of great mutual respect and often affection.

Empathy, not worry, is a primary function of caring.

Question: What happens when there is no empathy for the other - identify five consequences.

Reflection: Think of all the people in your life - make a list - then rate each relationship in terms of level of your AND their empathy - one is low and ten is high.

Action: Pick three people on your team and consciously seek to listen to their concerns and understand them better this week.

Unconscious Bias

When you realize that you create your own personal versions of other people within your consciousness, you start to become aware of your unconscious bias.

Your bias is not the same as others. Although, some days, it may seem so.

Bias are created by the beliefs and perceptions that are usually assimilated and learned in our younger years. They form the filter through which we perceive and create our version of others. Often extreme prejudices, which are not so unconscious, will skew our views of and about others.

'Unconscious' obviously means we are not aware this is happening.

And 'bias' means we are seeing and judging something about the other that others do not see.

In their crude and obvious forms our biases are arising whenever we 'argue' about the best team, the best political philosophy, the best brand etc.

Bias influences our decisions around issues like who gets hired and who gets a fast track promotion and who is seen to be not such a good performer when, in actuality they are doing fine!

To be free of unconscious bias it's necessary to become consciously aware of our unconscious tendencies.

Question: What are you biased towards in the areas of politics, sport, duties in the home, how your children should behave?

Reflection: In what ways do you think your biases have affected your decisions regarding the direction of your life?

Action: To raise awareness, initiate a discussion with the team this week around the topic, "What are our collective unconscious biases?"

Infinite Patience

The leader's role is not so much to 'get' the best out of others but to allow others to discover the best within themselves and give it expression.

This requires an environment in which it feels safe to express one's self. A context in which risk is encouraged and speaking one's mind is never discouraged.

Each person takes their own time to discover and bring the best of themselves to their work.

Recognizing their contribution, giving them permission to share their ideas knowing they will not be harshly judged and the opportunity to work with others in challenging ways, all help to encourage the best to emerge.

It's usually not a good idea to pressure and try to rush someone to discover their potential.

Exercise great patience with each one. When people notice this patience it helps them relax and that allows them to gather their strength to take that chance.

Perhaps this is why it has been said that 'infinite patience creates instant results'!

Question: In what ways do you currently create the space for the team to share what they really feel about what they do and could do?

Reflection: As you think of each team member what potential do you see in each and what might help them see the same in themselves?

Action: Sit with each member of the team in this coming week and ask them what might stretch them but not stress them i.e. what challenges would they welcome?

Consults Frequently

How often do you consult the team or individuals working for and around you?

Not one person has all the ideas, not one person makes all the best decisions, not one person has all the information.

On the good ship Enterprise, Captain Kirk was the one who tended to take the autocratic, dictatorial decisions whereas Captain Picard gathered his team and asked for information and suggestions.

Being a consulting leader means being perpetually curious and constantly questioning, as you are always digging for gold in the intellects of others.

As you do you make big statements in their eyes such as, "I recognize I do not have all the answers, I acknowledge I have much to learn, I value you and what you bring to the party".

Consulting your team collectively and individually, formally and informally, on small and large issues, is the wisest way of drawing on all the creative resources available to you.

Question: What happens to your relationship with someone when you consult them regularly?

Reflection: The best ideas are other people's ideas - when might this be true, when might this be false?

Action: What might be the obvious areas that each parson on your team could contribute more ideas/suggestions? List the people and then what might you seek their help with. Then reverse the list so that you ask the least obvious questions to someone who 'apparently' would not be able to help in that area. Experiment! Be surprised!

Respect Full

You understand the foundation of human relationship is respect.

If there is no respect for the other there is no real relationship and therefore little possibility of leadership.

Perhaps the most common mistake that managers make is to expect to be respected by virtue of their position.

And when they are not respected they withdraw their respect from the other.

But you are not dependent on the respect of others to bolster your self-respect.

You are still able to give respect even when others do not return it or when others make mistakes.

You are able to separate the person from the action, never losing your capacity to respect the other person, regardless of their actions in the past.

Question: Who do you find it hardest to give respct to and why do you think that is?

Reflection: Define respect.

Action: Visualise what you would do to affirm your respect for each person in your team this week. Be creative and find a different way for different people.

Cautious Inspiration

Why do people follow you?

The leader is cautious when someone follows them out of 'inspiration'.

While it can be a positive sign of the leader/follower relationship, the leader is able to sense if there is a subtle dependency that has developed within someone who is 'inspired' to follow.

With the recognition that no leader can inspire everyone all of the time, the enlightened leader seeks ways to assist the follower to find inspiration from within themselves.

This requires guiding, coaching and facilitating, as they help the follower to become more self-aware and restore the fullness of their self-respect (awareness of their value).

This helps them realize that what they think they see as inspirational in others is already present within themselves.

Question: Who in your team do you sense is always looking for inspiration from yourself or others?

Reflection: Why do people seem to need to be inspired to be motivated?

Action: Create a program among the team to explore and develop self-inspiration. Begin with a conversation around the meaning of inspiration, what is it exactly, how does it work precisely?

Trust Them

Do people trust you? Do you trust them? If you don't trust them will they easily trust you?

Will you wait for them to make the first move before you start to build trust with them?

Or have you realised that the leader in any relationship, especially the ones in the workplace, is the person who moves first.

Which moves would you make?

Perhaps by being more compassionate when you sense individuals on the team are going through a tough time in their life.

Perhaps when others are not as open to you as you might want them to be. So, you open-up to them, aware that it will be reciprocated eventually.

Perhaps when you stop to listen to their concerns and then do something about what is bothering them.

Perhaps by taking time, away from the workplace, to be with them, help them, support them, in some way in their life.

Perhaps by ensuring you are consistent in your responses.

Question: What does trust mean?

Reflection: If you think you are trust worthy why so, if not, why not.

Action: Research the meaning of trust and present your findings to the team. Then ask in what ways could 'we' build greater trust between and amongst ourselves as a team

Mike George

Mike is a senior member of the faculty of Cotrugli Business School

As a management tutor, facilitator and coach his specialist areas include Personal and Executive Development, Liberating Leadership and Managing with Emotional Intelligence.

He is an author of 15 books focused on cultivating self-awareness, emotional intelligence and personal enlightenment.

www.mikegeorgebooks.com

www.relax7.com

or email

mike@relax7.com

Cotrugli Business School

COTRUGLI Business School headquarters are located in Zagreb and Belgrade, with branch offices in Sofia, Bucharest, Ljubljana, Podgorica and Dubai.

In addition to MBA programs, COTRUGLI specializes in delivering customized in-house programs and Open Enrolment programs.

Zagreb: Buzinski prilaz 10, 10010, Zagreb, Croatia

Phone: +385 1 3706 270

Belgrade: Visegradska, Beograd, Serbia

Phone: +381 69 1190903

www.cotrugli.org

Lightning Source UK Ltd.
Milton Keynes UK
UKHW041450041118
331762UK00003B/10/P